HYGGE ·

The Secrets of the Hygge art towards a Stress-Free and Happier Life

DANIELLE KRISTIANSEN

CONTENTS

INTRODUCTION

Hygge, pronounced as "hoo-ga," is not as complicated as it sounds. It will benefit a lot of people, especially those who are often exposed to stress. This is
the primary reason why its popularity has gone
beyond its roots, which is Denmark.

Many books have been written and articles
published about the hygge lifestyle. It has also been
featured on many people's social media sites. Many
companies have capitalized on marketing products
related to this way of living, including blankets,
incense, candles, and many more.

This book aims to guide you about the process by
explaining what hygge is all about. It explains the
benefits of the process and how you can make it
work for you.

Anyone can adapt to the hygge lifestyle, even
those living in places where it doesn't snow. You only
have to focus on the factors to make your life less
stressful and a lot happier. This book offers tips and

techniques about how to include hygge in your everyday life, food and drinks, home and living, budgeting, and holiday seasons.

The best thing about hygge is that it is not restrictive about anything. It gives you freedom and happiness to pursue or eat whatever you want, for as long as they make you feel better and lighter.

Let's begin our Hygge journey!

CHAPTER 1

WHAT YOU NEED TO KNOW ABOUT HYGGE

It is more than a lifestyle. It is a culture. Hygge, pronounced as "hoo-ga," continues to invade many people's interests from all over the world. It all started after the word made it to the shortlist for Oxford's Word of the Year in 2016, which means that hygge is considered an expression that many people use and shows potential to have lasting cultural importance.

Many articles have come out about the topic from major publications, such as the Guardian and the New York Times between 2016 and 2017 alone. Plus, above 30 published books were released about the cozy lifestyle that, from then on, became no longer exclusive to Denmark. Major industries and businesses also utilized the barrage of information in marketing their products, including leisure items, blankets, candles, and many more.

Among the books published at the time had a three-time reprint before it was released. It was entitled "The Little Book of Hygge," a bestseller published in 26 countries. It was written by the Happiness Research Institute's founder, Meik Wiking.

Wiking describes hygge as being consciously cozy; it's about equality, gratitude, good food, indulgence, being together with the people you love, and all those things combined. The concept, for Wiking, is neither self-help nor a lifestyle. It is a significant part of the Danes' culture, which they consider part of their national DNA.

Many people who have adopted the culture consider it the art of creating a pleasant atmosphere. It has also been quoted as the "pursuit of everyday happiness."

It was during the time of Trump's presidential election in the US and Brexit in the United Kingdom when hygge reached an international level of fascination. The concept was fitting at such times when people were seeking togetherness and comfort. Many people seek the essence of hygge whenever uncertainties loom. It somehow gives people a pleasant feeling or a safe zone, no matter what is happening around them.

All About Feeling Good

Hygge promotes the feeling of contentment, something that seems so hard to attain as years go by. It believes that you feel good when you are cozy – while wrapped up in the soft cushions, having a nice cup of tea, or using warm slippers. It doesn't matter why you do it; what's more important is what you are feeling.

The term may have reached many people's consciousness in recent years, but The New Yorker reported something about it back in 1957. According to the report, the Copenhagen sidewalks were packed with hyggelige people, all smiling and lift their hats in acknowledging one another and strangers while giving them a look to make these people feel that they wanted to know more about them.

The hygge lifestyle is often compared to the idea of gezelligheid of the Dutch people and gemütlichkeit of the Germans. The term came from a Norwegian word that means wellbeing. In Denmark, hygge is used both as an adjective and a noun. America caught up with the trend in 2017, with Pinterest predicting that it would be one of the most sought-after trends in home décor that year.

The BBC reported that the Nordic winters paved the way for its people's adaptation of hygge to cope with the chilly weather. During wintertime, the average temperature is around 32 degrees, and the worst of the season can manifest through blackness for up to 17 hours per day. Since people have nothing to do outside, they have thought of ways to get comfortable and creative while staying indoors.

A lot of people attribute Denmark's frequent inclusion to the top 10 list of the United Nation's World Happiness Report to hygge. This international poll surveys citizens to self-evaluate their wellbeing. This proves that despite hygge allowing unhealthy eating, Denmark is not known for the fire hazards caused by often-lit fireplaces or people having diabetes for eating candies and sweets. They are known for happiness – something that many people would do anything to attain.

According to reports, Danes eat a lot of candy per capita, and they light more candles than any other nationalities in Europe. They do all these in pursuit of hygge. Wiking says that the key terms of hygge are an indulgence, savoring pleasures, and something sinful at times. It's about alcohol, hot chocolate, candy, and cake – sinful pleasures that give you a breather from the demands of healthy eating.

Wiking admitted that these foods might be bad for one's health, maybe one reason why Norwegians have a shorter life expectancy than the people in Sweden. They may be eating more unhealthy foods, but they are conscious about it, and they know the reason they are doing it – it makes them feel good and most important, it makes them happy.

You may already be doing hygge without realizing it. If you have ever decided to relax amid a pile of work, eat dinner as a whole family without anyone using a gadget, and while enjoying the conversation, or reading a good book as it rains, you are already doing hygge. It is the feeling of contentment at the simplest life pleasures.

∾

Seeking Comfort

Hygge is a refuge from the fast-paced and stressful life. It is gravitating towards anything that makes you feel light not only during the cold season but any time you feel like you need it. It doesn't have an English translation, but many people from all over the world have already adopted the lifestyle for how they perceive what hygge means.

It can mean different things for different people. The bottom line here is that you do it because it makes you feel happy. You do it not only to escape from the harshness of life but to learn to accept your truth and find ways to exist without focusing on negativities and learning how to manage your daily stress. Its definition will depend on one's interpretation. It can be all about managing stress for you, finding ways to enjoy the busy life for another, learning about how to become more comfortable no matter the situation for a different person, or doing all these things and more for yet another person. There is no right or wrong way of interpreting hygge; you can do anything that makes your life cozy, comfy, and happy.

It is a mindset of deliberately focusing on things that make you feel happier. It is the choices you make to improve your wellbeing and contentment. It is making time in doing the following with conscious effort because they make you feel good or you feel like they make you an hyggelige individual:

- Inviting some friends to your house for no particular reason and bond with them
- Cuddling in a warm blanket while watching a movie
- Making a meal from scratch and enjoying the food after or sharing it with a loved one
- Going outside to take a breather and go for a walk
- Dressing up in any way you feel most comfortable, like wearing something out of season, worn-out clothes, fuzzy socks, or sweatpants
- Sitting near the fireplace
- Lighting scented candles
- Brewing tea or coffee and enjoying your sip while it's still hot
- Curling up in bed doing nothing or while reading a book, you've wanted to finish

Hygge is doing the things that allow yourself to pause and take a break, and by doing so, you feel good and recharged after. These are the things that feel soothing and make you forget your daily hassles for a time. It allows you to enjoy your activities without being too dependent on technology.

The Global Interest in Hygge

The concept of hygge reminds many people of simplicity, something that becomes so rare as you become an adult and get caught up in the hustles and bustles of everyday life. One of the reasons why many people seek hygge is that it reminds them to look after themselves and be mindful of their happiness, mental and physical wellbeing as they go through life.

No matter how you work hard, you won't enjoy the fruits of your labor if you will get sick or easily succumb to burnout. Before you can love your work and the people around you, you must first learn to love yourself and exercise self-care.

Hygge reminds you about what you can do to deal with stress, but it doesn't stop there. It gives you many choices on what you can do at any moment you feel like it. It teaches you about the things you can do to make you feel good, depending on your personality. Hygge caters to introverts and extroverts. People of all ages can do it. It is something with a universal appeal that can only mean one thing – at the end of the day, people want to be happy.

The lifestyle is practical. It doesn't teach you to declutter your home by buying expensive storage stuff. It doesn't persuade you to go vegetarian or organic to live longer. It doesn't tell you to go on a cruise or enroll in an expensive yoga class to feel better. It promotes peace, comfort, and indulgence without breaking the bank.

Going Hygge During Summer

Hygge doesn't have rules. You can do it anytime, no matter what the season is. More than a lifestyle, it is a state of mind where you imbibe simplicity and enjoyment. While there are many things "hygge" you can do during wintertime, you can also do a lot of things when the weather is warm.

Here are some ideas of how you can go hygge during summer:

- Spend time outdoors. Make the most of the season by enjoying the outdoors. You can go for a walk while soaking up in the warmth of the sun. You can ride a bike, go on a canoe or boat ride, or hike. You can also spend quality time with friends and gather around a bonfire on a beach. No matter what you do, you have to make the most of the experience and enjoy it.

- Get cozy. Find ways to get cozy even while the weather is hot by swapping the things you do during the winter with anything that fits the season. Change the warm blankets and beddings with lightweight nylons and breathable linens. Wear tank tops or shirts instead of wooly socks and a sweater. You can still enjoy scented candles but do not light as many pieces as you do when the weather is cold.

- Pick or buy fresh flowers. It is the season when many flowers are in bloom. You can share your garden with your friends or neighbors. You can also buy flowers and put them all over your house. Many people feel happy and lighter whenever they see and smell fresh flowers. You can also share the happiness by giving out flowers to acquaintances and people you love.

- Check out a farmer's market or go to a local festival. Summer is an excellent time to enjoy the company of other people while enjoying food and music.

- Buy a hammock and take a nap whenever you feel like it. It's relaxing and a good way to beat the heat while swinging gently

in a hammock as you take some time to
rest.

- Have a barbecue in the backyard or go on a
  picnic. Enjoy the grass along with the
  warm weather. Share the experience with
  the people you love. Savor the food while
  keeping up with your friends and loved
  ones.

A Lifestyle Appealing to All Senses

The hygge lifestyle affects all your senses. It is not
only cozy and comfortable but most of all, it's heart-
warming. Here's a look at how hygge benefits your
body's major senses:

1. Sense of taste

While this kind of lifestyle does not prohibit
anything when it comes to food, you have to be
mindful of what you take into your system all the
time. The purpose is to enjoy, and you can only do
that when you remain healthy despite the lifestyle
changes. It is okay to allow yourself to indulge in
sweets and junk foods every once in a while or even
often, but you have to do it in a way that you get to
enjoy and savor what you eat and not having to
worry about the health consequences of your actions.
There are no rules since hygge doesn't want you to

feel restricted, so everything you do, you have to think about how it will benefit you not only in a brief moment but in the long run.

Some of the hygge lifestyle staples include hearty meals, healthy treats, wine, and warm beverages. It allows you to enjoy mindful indulgence not only in the food you eat but the process of making it. For example, you may want to try bread making and get awed by how the dough rises after several minutes to hours or how the house smells bread after baking. You can also try cooking popcorn in a pot or simmer a stew for long hours. Aside from basking into the process, the best way is to enjoy what you have prepared with the people you love. You can also try asking them to help in the kitchen every once in a while.

2. Sense of touch

Hygge is mostly about what makes you feel good and warm. It's about getting cozy and not feeling guilty about even when you are seen in public on your wooly socks or a hyggebukser or sweatpants. All these things can be felt physically and literally. To add to the experience, you can try more hygge activities you can touch, such as feeling the twigs or snow beneath your feet, knitting, or reading printed magazines or books.

3. Sense of sight

Hygge improves the aesthetics you surround yourself with. It softens a room and makes the ambiance warmer. You allow your eyes to enjoy the open flames or flickering candles, soft bulbs or string of lights, or other visuals, such as a good film, outdoor sceneries, or reading a book.

It gives you some time off from the things that might harm your sense of sight, including laptop, tablet, or phone, anything that connects you to the outside world and disconnects you from all the coziness. Some say that hygge sort of gives them a digital detox. It's like seeking comfort and utmost relaxation for some time to recharge, to bond with the people you love, before going back to your usual routine.

4. Sense of hearing

You can find hygge playlists on popular online music streaming sites. These are the sounds that feel light and soft to the ears. They can also be anything that makes you feel soothing, such as silence, sounds of nature, laughter, and conversation with friends and family.

5. Sense of smell

With hygge, you can choose the scents that will remind you of good memories or people. They can be comforting and joyous scents that will bring in the holiday vibes, such as allspice, vanilla, or cinnamon. You can also get comforted by the smell of food, such as savory meals, coffee, or decadent treats. The scent can come from nature, the trees, or the night air.

Hygge and Relationships

While there are times you'd feel comfortable and relieved from stress when you are on your own, most of the time with hygge, you'd seek the company of other people, especially the ones you care about.

The original purpose of hygge was to help the Scandinavian people survive the harsh winter without becoming victims of depression and starvation. It also instilled the importance of other people – your loved ones and people in the community or building social relationships not only to survive but, more importantly, to thrive.

Social support is one of the categories being looked upon by the World Report of Happiness in ranking different nations according to people's life's satisfaction. It is one of the gauges used alongside with workplace environment and economic stability.

People with strong social support tend to have a higher sense of self-worth and a sense of belonging. They also feel more secure knowing that they have people to turn to whenever in need and that they are surrounded by those who care for them.

The Opposite of Hygge

Before learning more about what you can do to obtain hygge, here's a list of the common things people do that are not considered hygge:

1. Buying trendy things. America and UK may have already caught up using hygge in marketing their products, a different concept from the original hygge, which is to stay away from accumulating material things. The original idea is to create an atmosphere to be happy and not depend on material and expensive items. You can reach hygge by merely enjoying the simplest life's pleasures.

2. Staying indoors all winter on your own. You don't have to hibernate in your nook during winter all by yourself, even though you take the time to enjoy a good book or sip hot chocolate to keep you warm. You have to share the happiness. So even if the weather is freezing, you can schedule a time to get outdoors to see the view and meet people. You must also spend time with the people you care about, those that make you happy.

3. Doing away with strict rules. Hygge encourages simplicity and for people to give in to what makes them happy, even if that means grabbing the last slice of cake. It enables you to have fun and refrain from complaining. If you feel like complaining about the bad weather, refrain yourself from doing so, and instead, have a cup of tea or light some candles, and enjoy the moment. You can also cook up something and invite your friends to share

the food while catching up and having a good conversation.

CHAPTER 2

THE BENEFITS OF HYGGE AND
HOW IT RELATES TO HAPPINESS

Hygge promotes the opposite of the lifestyle many people of today have. It allows you to embrace the good and block the negativities. Its primary purpose is to allow you to feel and experience happiness.

The hygge way of living also offers the following benefits:

1. Physical

When you feel the presence of comfort and safety, both your body and mind get relaxed. For a time, you will give in to the soothing pleasures of the hygge lifestyle. Your body can rest for a while from scanning your surroundings for threats, and as a result, you will experience the following health benefits:

- Not easily tempted to try unhealthy vices, such as drugs and alcohol

- Being conscious about self-care
- Less stress
- Weight regulation
- Quality sleep

2. Emotional

Hygge encourages you to arrange and decorate your home so that you will feel at peace and calm whenever you are in it. Having a cozy living space benefits all your senses. It makes you feel safe and comfortable. It allows you to understand the essence of being at "home." By doing so, you will find it easier to let your guard down and be more open to connecting with the other people inside.

Here are some of the emotional benefits of hygge living:

- Being more grateful
- Practicing self-compassion
- Practicing mindfulness
- Reduced stress
- Becoming more optimistic
- Realizing your self-worth
- Reduced risk from anxiety and depression

3. Social

It becomes easier to connect with other people

when you feel emotionally safe and stable. You become more approachable, and you start building and nurturing relationships. Hygge puts more emphasis on one's connection with loved ones, friends, and family. You feel the need to spend more time with the people who matter to you. By doing so, you become more emotionally healthy and more confident about yourself, especially when you are around other people. You become more open to your weaknesses and vulnerabilities. You embrace them and find ways to improve or change.

You will gain the following social benefits when you practice hygge:

- Reduced time in using social media
- Becoming better with your personal relationships
- Developing new social connections
- Increased intimacy
- Learning how to trust
- Feeling comfortable and safe
- Having your attention on togetherness

4. Wellness

Hygge is not only about getting cozy all the time. It pushes you to do the activities you enjoy that you won't feel like they are chores. You will do things because they make you feel good. By doing so, your overall wellness will improve, and you will have lower stress levels. According to research, the people from the countries that first practiced hygge, Finland, Denmark, and Sweden, were among the places with the least stressed people.

Hygge is not solely about eating or sitting around a fire. It can inspire you to follow a regular exercise regimen as long as you enjoy whatever you are doing. You can practice stress-relieving exercise indoors or go outdoors and try hiking or ice skating. By doing so, you will feel lighter and will have a sense of improved self-esteem.

Despite allowing hygge enthusiasts to eat sweets and drink beer, somehow, you will manage to do this in ways that will not affect your health. You will only reach for the treats to enjoy the good things in life without the guilt. One satisfactory proof of this claim is that the number of obese people in Sweden is lower than the percentage in Britain.

More about the Benefits of the Lifestyle

You may be wondering how a lifestyle like hygge is capturing the interests of people from around the world. It is now applied in many homes, businesses, and there is also a college in the UK that teaches the Danish hygge.

Most people who have developed a keen interest in hygge boast about its influence on their health and wellbeing. Here are some of the more specific benefits of the popular lifestyle:

1. Hygge teaches you about mindful eating.

Hygge prompts you to take care of yourself, and a big part of it includes eating what you want. More than the food, it is vital to enjoying the process of eating. You have to practice mindful eating or indulging your taste buds by enjoying every bite and chewing your food slowly to achieve this. This way, you won't restrict yourself from eating anything, but you won't overeat as well because of how you're doing things. To enjoy the process, even more, you may want to share your meals with friends or families.

Go hygge by preparing a pot of soup and ask your friends and family to share it with you while enjoying small talks near the fireplace.

2. It calms your mind.

The lifestyle encourages you to focus on the present and enjoy every second of it. It serves as a pause or breather from your busy schedule. It becomes a refuge or something you look forward to experiencing after several days of working too hard. It makes you seek, even every once in a while, how hyggelige feels like. Hyggelige is the adjective term of hygge for doing nothing.

Go hygge by turning off all your gadgets, replacing lights with scented candles, and enjoying a long salt bath mixed with several drops of your favorite essential oils. Moisturize after while talking to your body positively. Sip a hot tea or read a good book, and have a quality and peaceful sleep.

3. The lifestyle promotes sound sleep.

There are many rituals you do in hygge that result in an improved quality of sleep. It encourages you to turn away from the screens and disconnect from your social media sites before sleeping at night. Instead, you will focus on activities that will relax your mind, such as scrolling through old photo albums, preparing a nice tea, or having a good conversation with your partner. All these are hygge, and they will help you sleep soundly and feel well-rested and recharged upon waking up.

4. It helps in relaxing your muscles.

Most of the hyggelige techniques promote relax-ation. You will only realize how much burden you've been carrying after experiencing the results of taking a well-deserved rest and a nightly pampering. It will not only feel good and relaxing but, in many ways, healing.

5. The lifestyle helps you focus on the people that matter and strengthen your relationship with them.

Hygge is not all about "me time." It combines the time you allot for yourself and the precious moments you share with those you care about by spending quality time together. There are many things you can do to go hygge with these people you love.

You can set a date for a movie night with your friends. Set the ambiance of your home by lighting candles and turning off the main lights. Prepare hot tea, popcorn, or cheese slices that you will share with them as you enjoy the movie.

You can also set a date night with your partner. This is something often overlooked, especially when life gets busier or after having children. You have to spend quality time talking, bonding, cuddling, or anything you will both enjoy. Make it more hyggelige by lighting candles and putting on romantic music. If time permits, you can set your dates off to places you've always want to visit or bonding over the activities you both enjoy. The idea here is to spend time catching up and expressing your love for one another.

Hygge and Happiness

Among the many benefits of hygge, which attracts many people the most is how it affects your emotions, how it makes you feel lighter and happy. Happiness is something so important, but its meaning varies from person to person. You may find happiness in life's simplest pleasures, while another person's happiness lies in splurging. Hygge is defined as "the state of being happy" by the Oxford English Dictionary.

It still may sound surreal, but it stated a good point, which is it is not a trait, but a state, which can change and isn't long-lasting. Happiness can also be an external or internal experience or both. It is not to be confused with bliss or ecstasy, but more of the feeling of being content.

In positive psychology, happiness is referred to as subjective well-being or SWB, but the definition is still undergoing many debates and discussions. A 2005 research related happiness to the following factors in positive psychology:

- It's a result of the different cumulated reactions gathered through time.
- It is a recollection of a person's emotional experiences in the past.
- It is a global valuation of all life's facets.

While happiness is often interchanged with plea-sure, especially in literature, the two have distinct differences. Pleasure is more of what you feel in the moment and sensory-based emotions for various reasons, such as getting a compliment, eating your favorite food, or making love.

Happiness is more stable despite being temporary, like pleasure. The latter can come and go in a few seconds, but the happiness lasts longer. You can also bring the feeling back when you recall what caused it.

There have been a lot of different theories about happiness that have varying opinions but agree on specific points, including the following:

- Happiness can come from various sources.
- It rarely happens that you obtain happiness from the pursuit and accomplishment of pleasure.
- Around 10 to 50 percent of people's happiness can be due to genetic factors.
- Happiness is not a long-term trait; it is not stable or fleeting.
- People like the feeling of happiness, and it is something beneficial.

Many studies have found out that good relationships play a significant factor in a person's happiness. The other essential factors that contribute to your overall jovial state include the following:

- Experiencing positive emotions
- Moral values
- Social relationships

- Family
- Physical well-being
- Labor market status
- Individual income

People tend to be happier when they feel happy about their close relationships, which include their family, significant other, and closest friends. Since you have control over these relationships, it only proves the point that it is possible to learn how to be happier.

This is where hygge can help you – become happier by embracing the kind of lifestyle that allows you to indulge, take a breather, and get cozy even every once in a while.

Denmark, the country of origin of the hygge life-style, consistently ranks in the list of the world's happiest countries. Researchers say that this can be attributed to other factors aside from hygge, including the Danes' access to premium health care and high-quality education. They also have low levels of public corruption and have a stable government.

Hygge has various definitions relating the life-style to coziness, but it can be better defined as inten-tional intimacy. You can only achieve this state when you have harmonious, balanced, and safe shared experiences. It can be a simple gathering with your family or sharing a cup of tea with a loved one in front of a fireplace.

In attending Danish social events, it would be

impolite to say that they were hyggelige because
these people make it a point to give off such a vibe.
You can compliment a Danish host by saying that the
event was hyggeligt, which is equivalent to saying
you had a good time. Homes and other spaces can
also be described as hyggelige when they are deco-
rated and arranged in ways to make them more
homey and comfortable.

Hygge plays a crucial part in the people's sense of
well-being in Denmark. The lifestyle promotes trust
and egalitarianism. It allows the people to make
room for friendship a wall to defend them against
stress.

The US doesn't have a cultural equivalent to
hygge even though the country also places high
importance on individualism. Other countries with
similar concepts to hygge include Germany's
gemütlichkeit, Netherlands' gezenlligheid, Sweden's
mysig, and Norwegians' koselig.

The happiness of the people in the US is generally
associated with income. It makes one wonder though
since the levels of people's happiness in the US have
been continuously decreasing despite the decline in
the country's unemployment rate and the continuous
rise of its GDP.

The problem lies in hygge's belief in the importance of building trust and intimacy with others.
Aside from the continuing problem with income
inequality in the US, its media and government get a
decreasing rate of the people's trust. People also tend
to lack interpersonal trust, something that the

hyggelige people have mastered and keep on improving.

Boosting Your Happiness with Hygge

No matter where in the world you are, you can try the different hyggelige ways to boost your happiness. You can begin with these five:

1. Always be grateful

Hygge encourages you to focus on the present. This way, you will appreciate what's happening "now" and acknowledge the good things no matter how simple they seem to be instead of taking them for granted. Being grateful brings in more positivity in your life. This prompts you to build more intimate relationships and look after yourself.

Hygge is an experience and something that cannot be bought. It's an atmosphere you create, the connection you make with people, your conscious effort to take things slow, and by showing your appreciation for yourself and everything that surrounds you. In hygge, it's the little things that count, although there are times when you'd feel like buying certain things that appeal to you. This kind of lifestyle teaches you to focus on the simplest pleasures and show your gratitude.

2. Learn how to take things slow

As you adopt the hygge lifestyle in your everyday

life, you will learn how to take your time to enjoy things or the process. It is ideal to focus on the moments, including the smallest ones that bring about happiness.

These moments are distinct and must not be forced or rushed. It would be hard to appreciate something if you keep on thinking about what will happen next. You have to learn how to focus on what is happening at the moment to savor the experience. According to science, people are happier when they are mindful, and their attention is captured by what is happening "here and now."

3. Connect with your family and friends

According to research, a person's happiness heavily relies on the quality of their relationships. It is crucial to follow the hygge way of bonding with your loved ones to make the relationship stronger and always make time to see them in person and spend time with them.

Hygge will teach you about the ways to connect with the people that matter and strengthen your bond with them. You can do this in an informal and cozy setting, where you will share the fun of food preparation, eating together, talking, laughing, and getting updated with one another. Bonding doesn't have to be grand. The essential thing is that you are all present and that you enjoy the atmosphere and the company.

You can also expand your social connections by

getting yourself involved in a local community. You can take part in groups that share your interests, such as book club, gardening group, sports, or choir. This will give you a sense of belonging while boosting your happiness and well-being.

4. Enjoy nature

Connecting with nature can have a positive impact on your body and mind. Hygge doesn't limit you to the comforts of a book shop, coffee house, or your home. You can do it anywhere, including the outdoors with nature, any time. You can go skiing or sledding in winter, enjoy picnics, hiking, or camping in summer, or bask in the beauty of the plants' blossoms in spring. It can also be anytime when you want to go outside to smell the fresh air and enjoy the view.

5. Practice kindness all the time

It pays to be kind to other people and most especially, to yourself. Hygge allows you to seek activities, places, and people that will make you feel restored, relaxed, connected, and happy. It gives practical reasons why you need to slow down and do the activities that others may disregard as lazy or unimportant. You indulge in pleasurable activities without feeling guilty.

～

The Rules to Achieve Danish Happiness

What is it about hygge that makes it more possible for people to be happy? The term, hygge, doesn't translate to other languages, and it's not merely a term or a word. It's a way of living, an action, a feeling. It's not only an idea but more of a mood.

Here are the essential rules to experience hygge and the happiness and sense of self that come with it:

Rule number 1: Dim the lights

Denmark leads the countries with the highest consumption of candles in Europe, with every person said to be consuming 6 kilos of candle wax each year. The second on the list is Austria, with each person consuming 3 kilos of candle wax annually. The majority of the Danish population agrees that candles are essential to hygge. Twenty-eight percent of them light candles every day, and almost 75 percent do so at least once a week.

Rule number 2: Get together

Hygge doesn't mean that you can barge into a circle of people, and they will accept you with open arms. Getting together has to be a regular thing. Even if you move to Denmark, it will take time and lots of effort before you can find people to hygge with.

It is not about big parties, but more of a small celebration of people getting together to celebrate security, comfort, and trust. Only 11 percent of the Danish people think that you can hygge with five or more people. About 57 percent of them agree that 3 to 4 are the ideal numbers of people to celebrate hygge with. No matter what your preference is for the number of people, the more crucial part is not only to keep it low but to have the hygge gathering at least once a week.

Rule number 3: Turn your home into a house into a hyggelige home

Hygge is all about the right atmosphere. About 71 percent of Danish homes create a specific area where it feels warm, cozy, and beautiful, which they call "Hyggekrog." Most of them have a fireplace at home, and their Hyggekrog has blankets, candles, and books. They are also meticulous about furniture design, and they adore the designs that fit into their lifestyle.

Rule number 4: Be present in the "now"

Hygge encourages you to take things slow even once in a while, disconnect from the online world and be more present in what's happening at the present moment and who you are with.

It gives you a chance to breathe, relax, and for the time being, forget about your problems or deadlines. It allows you to drop the seriousness and enjoy the company of your friends and family.

. . .

Rule number 5: Dress in comfortable clothes

Go casual as hygge is all about comfort and warmth, so you can also put on a scarf, gloves, or a knitted sweater or jumper. Also, make sure that you have a blanket ready, especially when the weather is freezing.

Rule number 6: Eat what you want and enjoy

Danes love cookies, meat, and anything home-cooked and tasty. A perfect get together wouldn't be complete without their traditional open sandwich, called Smørrebrød. They also love tea and coffee and actually made it in the fourth spot of the biggest coffee drinkers worldwide.

CHAPTER 3
HYGGE IN MINIMIZING STRESS

You will hear this a lot as you learn more about hygge – less stress, which is an essential benefit of the lifestyle. While stress is not always bad, it becomes unhealthy and even detrimental to health when you are often exposed to stressors or the causes of stress.

Hygge does not eliminate stress, as it is impossible to do. What happens is that you learn to adapt to the kind of lifestyle where you will have less exposure to stress and develop your skills in dealing with it. Hygge makes you accept that stress is not a problem but rather a part of life. It only becomes a problem when you look at it that way.

Stress is your body's response to anything it sees as a threat. When your body perceives something as a stressor or cause of stress, your body's nervous system automatically releases a flood of stress hormones to help you cope with the feeling. These hormones include adrenaline and cortisol, which prompt you to do something. It makes your blood pressure rise and your heartbeat faster. As the stress levels become higher, your muscles become tighter and your senses sharper.

You become more attentive when faced with a stressor. Your tension grows, and you become capable of doing things faster all of a sudden. Your body enters the flight or fight mode when it perceives something as a threat. It protects you in a way, and it can even save your life, especially during emergencies.

A good example is when a person suddenly crosses the street while you are driving. Stress will make you alert that will immediately put your body in action, so you will immediately slam on the brakes to avoid the accident.

Stress can also help you overcome difficult situations. It gives you the courage to come up on stage despite being nervous or go on with your performance even after making a mistake. Stress helps you stay focused and alert in an important meeting or study despite the temptations around you. In general, stress helps you rise above the challenges.

It only becomes unhealthy when you allow stress to affect your mind and body negatively. When it becomes too much, your body will find it hard to differentiate whether you are faced with a daily stressor or a life-threatening situation. It becomes too much when it keeps on happening over and over again.

Because your system is confused, it repeatedly goes into a fight or flight mode. As a result, your health suffers from high blood pressure and faster heart rate, which can cause other health problems, which include the following:

- Heart ailment
- Stroke
- Muscle pains
- Lower immunity
- Skin problems
- Weight disorders
- Depression
- Sleep disorder
- Digestive problem

Minimizing Stress the Hygge Way

The hygge lifestyle suits those who want to minimize the levels of stress they face every day. Since it is bound to happen and stress is part of life, the best thing you can do to help yourself is to learn how to respond or handle it, including the causes.

This won't happen overnight, but the process will become faster as you get more engaged in hygge.

Here are some effective quick relief techniques for all your body senses done in a manner suitable for the hygge lifestyle:

1. Sense of sight

- Imagine or visualize images that calm your nerves, especially when you are stressed out. You can also place images or things around you that make you feel calmer and lighter.
- Display images of your loved ones or captured photos of unforgettable memories at your work desk.
- Go out for a walk, relax, and enjoy the peacefulness and you bask in the beauty that surrounds you. It can be on a beach, garden, park, or even around the neighborhood or in your backyard.
- Bring in life from the outdoors inside your office or homes, such as flowers or plants, to make the ambiance more appealing and alive.
- Close your eyes whenever stress hits you and imagine yourself at your favorite place, like at the beach or your childhood home. Try to relax as you take your mind to the place when you would rather be.
- Fill your surroundings with the colors that make you feel good. You can paint the walls or wear clothes in colors that make you feel light.

2. Sense of hearing

- Experiment or remember the sounds that make your mood lighter, such as listening to your kind of music or singing your favorite song.
- Listen closely to the sounds of nature as you relax in the beach, park, or your backyard.
- You can place a miniature of a fountain at your work desk or hang a wind chime.
- You can also do vocal toning if you don't have a talent for singing or you are tone-deaf. Sit straight, close your eyes, and make the sound of a long "umm," like how it's done in meditation and yoga. Listen to the sound you're making and observe how your body reacts to it. Change the speed, volume, and pitch until you find the right tone that soothes your nerves.

3. Sense of smell

- Surround yourself with scents that are refreshing and energizing. Look for the kinds of scents that calm your nerves whenever you are stressed out.
- Dab yourself with your favorite perfume or cologne.
- Go outdoors and breathe in the smell of fresh air.

- Stock on candles with your favorite scents, and light them when you need to feel calm, or you can also burn incense.
- Use a lavender-scented fabric conditioner on your bedsheets and pillowcases. The scent will help in making you feel lighter and help in making your fall asleep faster.

4. Sense of touch

- Wear clothes that feel comfortable on your skin, made from materials that allow your skin to breathe.
- Wrap your body in a warm blanket whenever you are alone and longing to be hugged.
- Add some drops of your favorite essential oil in the water and soak in a hot bath.
- Play with your pets and get comforted when you touch them.
- Give yourself a quick massage on your hands, back, or neck whenever you feel like you need it.

5. Sense of taste

- Be mindful of the taste of your food and

how you chew. This will help you enjoy your food and avoid overeating.
- Savor the taste of your coffee or tea by slowly sipping while they're hot.
- Chew your food or treats slowly.

6. Sense of movement

- When you have experienced something in the past, the tendency is to develop the habit of shutting down when faced with stress. To deal with the behavior and help yourself relax in the process, you have to prompt your body to move.
- Jump up and down or jog in place, or you can also dance.
- Stretch your body and feel the limbs and your muscles flex.
- Walk, move, or pace back and forth.
- Squeeze a stress ball in your hand until your muscles relax, and you feel calmer.

Hygge and Stress

You need to be present at the moment to fully experience hygge. You have to feel at ease with yourself and the world around you. To deal with stress the hygge way, you have to channel your feelings towards the factors that comfort you.

The lifestyle is an ideal coping mechanism to diffuse the bomb that stress has triggered inside of you. It is not enough to say that you will stop feeling stressed. You have to take a breather and try to slow things down, which is what hygge is all about. Your goal is to combat stress and regain control over your life.

You may already know about the benefits of the techniques listed below but tend to forget to apply them whenever needed. The following ways are suited to the hygge lifestyle and are effective ways to defeat stress and its causes:

1. Laugh

Laughing is a great way to relieve stress, so make it a habit to laugh even when there is nothing particularly funny. You can try to remember a funny situation or joke or watch funny video clips online. Forced laughter may sound unnatural at first, but it will sound more natural as you continue doing it. Laughing boosts the release of endorphins in the brain, and it also helps in relaxing your muscles.

. . .

2. Body scan meditation

This exercise helps in making you aware of all your body sensations. First, you have to choose a quiet spot where you will lie or sit comfortably with your eyes closed. Focus on the different parts of your body, beginning at your feet to your head. Scan each body part and focus on how they feel. Look for the parts with the most tension and use the power of your mind to release the tension and make the stress go away. Open your eyes once you are done, breathe deeply, and focus on the present. Feel the changes that happened to your body, to how you feel, once you are done with the meditation.

3. Deep breathing exercise

It's good to practice this exercise whenever stress hits wherever you are. Close your eyes and focus your attention on your breathing and nothing else. Be attentive to how your body reacts to each inhale and exhale. Do this for a few minutes before opening your eyes to come back to the present. You will notice how it makes your load lighter and your mood brighter.

4. Sleep

You will be amazed at how getting sufficient sleep can relieve you of the heaviness and grumpiness you feel inside. Just make sure that you don't oversleep because it can worsen your mood. Help yourself improve your sleep quality by playing soothing music, diffusing comforting scents, wearing comfortable clothes, and letting go of your worries as you allow yourself to fall into a slumber.

5. Dance

Dancing, a form of exercise, helps in releasing and pumping up the endorphins to your system. It will make you feel better and happier.

6. Spending time in the kitchen

The kitchen is among many people's favorite part of their homes. It feels comforting and warm, even when you don't do anything but to relax and smell the aroma coming from food and ingredients. If you are a good cook, you will also find activities such as mixing, cooking, and baking therapeutic.

7. Clean

Cleaning at the beginning of the day is a form of exercise that can boost your mood and energy, which you will carry throughout the day. It can also help relieve stress, especially when you are the kind of person who can't stand mess and dirt.

· · ·

8. Making your home a sanctuary

You can redecorate or arrange your house in a manner that you'd look forward to coming home each day. You can change the paint into your favorite color, display photos, or accents that feel comforting to look at, or diffuse your favorite scents before leaving in the morning.

9. Swimming

This activity, which is also a good form of exercise, effectively decreases the levels of your body's stress hormones. You can do this at the start of each day or before you hit your bed at night.

10. Always appreciate yourself

Stop worrying and start focusing on your positive qualities and achievements, no matter how small they are. Other people will find it easier to appreciate your efforts when they see that you are proud of what you've done.

11. Listening to music

Music has a soothing power linked to one's emotions, which can be effective in reducing stress. It relaxes the body and mind, especially when you listen to quiet and slow classical music.

Aside from exploring your emotions, music acts

as a distraction, preventing the mind from wandering and thinking about anything that might trigger stress. Classical music is the most calming to listen to, but you can also choose what to play depending on your preference.

It is normal to feel like not wanting to listen to music when stressed out, thinking that it's just a waste of time. You have to fight the feeling and make an effort to do the activity. You will only become more productive when your stress levels are low, and music can help achieve that. You will find various hygge music playlists on many online platforms.

12. Massage

Massage is a therapeutic way to reduce stress and body pains. It will also make you feel comfortable, relaxed, and cozy, making it a proper hygge step. To relieve stress, the most common types of massage used include therapeutic, Swedish, and deep tissue massage.

A therapeutic massage relaxes you by applying gentle pressure on body areas with soft tissues. This technique boosts the blood flow at areas of the body where stress is coming from. As a result, your body produces more positive hormones, such as dopamine, serotonin, and endorphins, which alleviate stress by helping you achieve the utmost relaxation. The increased blood flow also helps make the body tissue more elastic by increasing the muscles' temperature. It prevents the formation of muscular knots and reduces body tension.

Swedish is a massage technique that manipulates the muscles to help a person relax mentally and physically. As the muscles stretch, the body's tension and tightness get eased, and both the mental and physical stress is reduced.

A deep tissue massage focuses on the deeper layer of tissues and muscle fibers. It helps in loosening up the muscles to increase their movement, alleviate pains, and reduce stress.

∼

Beat Stress through Yoga

Yoga is a practical meditation technique with similarities to hygge, such as it helps you relax and calm down. The practice has changed through time and adapted to the needs of its followers. Its main goal is to unite the inner and outer qualities of life.

It is not a religious system, but certain spiritual practices include yoga. It is predominantly taught as a system of exercises and physical poses that aim to improve your well-being and health in general.

The practice includes a variety of techniques and poses targeted to get you to the point that you feel one with the universe. This is done by unifying your mind, spirit, and body. Once done, you will attain the best kind of relaxation and enlightenment.

. . .

Aside from having similar goals to hygge, yoga also offers the following benefits:

1. It makes you more flexible, which you will notice after a time of practicing the exercise, including its most challenging poses. If you intend to learn it on your own, make sure that you listen to your body with each movement. Never force yourself in doing poses perfectly and only reach at points when it still feels comfortable. Flexibility will come through time, but you have to ensure safety as you perform the poses as a beginner.

2. It improves your body posture, which can also reflect on your health. Poor posture can lead to pains in the muscles, back, neck, and joints. Slumping too often can lead to the spine's degenerative diseases.

3. Yoga makes the bones and muscles stronger. As you last in practicing yoga poses, you will learn how to lift your own weight. It results in many health benefits, including the reduced risk of osteoporosis and lower stress levels. It also keeps the calcium in the bones intact, resulting in healthier and stronger bones. Yoga makes the muscles stronger and protects you from health issues, such as back pain and arthritis.

· · ·

4. Yoga boosts your overall health and addresses your emotional and spiritual well-being. There are certain times in life when you'd feel at a loss no matter what you do. This is where you can use both hygge and yoga – to allow you to breathe, concentrate, and feel recharged after.

5. Doing yoga regularly will make your spine more flexible to enable you to perform the more complicated twists, forward, and backbends. It also boosts your blood flow, which aids in supplying your system with enough oxygen. It also decreases your risk of suffering from heart ailments and stroke.

6. Yoga protects you from depression. It clears your mind and keeps you fit. A big part of yoga involves concentration. It encourages you to seek silence and stay focused throughout the exercise. This may not be easy initially, but you'll get used to it through the days.

7. It helps in improving your balance. Yoga boosts your system's proprioception or the ability to feel where your physical body is and what it is doing. Poor proprioception is often caused by back pains, knee problems, and old age. While you may feel wobbly at the beginning of the practice, you will get

used to the process and have a better balance through continued training.

8. Yoga helps in releasing tension in your limbs. You may not be aware of your habits and mannerisms that are already causing chronic tension and muscle fatigue. They include the consistent facial expressions you do when staring at your computer screen and other gadgets, the way you grip the steering wheel while driving or how you hold the phone when talking to someone. You will only become aware of the problem once you begin to feel the pains. Yoga will teach you how to control and relax your muscles and release the tension before it hurts.

9. The practice boosts your immune system. Certain yoga poses require muscle contraction and stretching, which will increase the drainage of your lymph. Through this, your lymphatic system will be able to fight off infections and cancerous cells and get rid of harmful toxins.

10. Yoga will boost your self-esteem and self-confidence. It prompts you to set aside the negativities and focus on the positive aspects of your life. It will help you develop a firm belief that you can be whatever you want to be, which will inspire you to always give your best.

Yoga in Dealing with Stress

Stress becomes a problem when it happens all the time. It can develop into something chronic and lead to other worse health conditions. Your body will find it harder to cope with stress when you don't exercise. This is where yoga can help you - it teaches you how to manage stress by using your inner strength.

You can begin by doing daily yoga exercises, meditation, and breathing techniques. Through regular practice, your mind will learn how to calm down when you feel overwhelmed. Meditation will teach you to tap your inner resources to become happier and more fulfilled.

Yoga is a mind and body practice, bringing peace and calmness through mental and physical disciplines. Its three core components are poses, breathing, and meditation. Yoga poses as a series of movements intended to increase your flexibility. Yoga will teach you how to control your breathing, which will help in monitoring your body and clearing your mind. Meditation, which is integrated into the practice, helps you become more aware of the present. This is something similar to the practice of hygge, which prompts you to savor each moment and seize the day.

Yoga is generally safe, but it is best to consult your doctor and ask their advice about pursuing the practice if you are suffering from any of the following health conditions:

- Herniated disk
- Severe osteoporosis
- Health problems that can cause blood clots
- Glaucoma and other eye problems
- Pregnancy
- A severe problem with balance and posture
- Unregulated blood pressure

It is easier and safer to begin yoga practice under the supervision of a qualified trainer. You can also start on your own if you can't find one, but make sure that you read and study everything you need to know about the practice before you begin.

Start slow and stick with the easy movements when you are a beginner. Stretch your body but don't push it when you are already feeling pain and discomfort. You will eventually get better with the movements as your body becomes more flexible.

Here are some of the easy yoga poses for beginners you can try to deal with stress, and as part of your shift towards the hygge lifestyle:

1. Revolved Lunge

This is a detoxifying yoga pose that involves twisting, causing your internal organs to wring out, giving your chest more room to breathe by the end of the pose. Start on a regular lunge with your hands down. Twist to the right as you step your left foot backward, which will end you up doing a high lunge pose. Keep your weight stable as you sustain the pose and gently reach through your back heel. Bring your hands to Anjali Mudra (similar to a prayer position) in front of your chest, and twist your body to the right.

Press your elbow outside of your knee while keeping your hands in a prayer position in front of your chest. If this pose is still challenging for you as a beginner, you can keep your one hand in a prayer position and extend your other arm. If you are finding it difficult to sustain your balance, you can keep the back of your knee down with your toes tucked underneath.

You are not expected to perfect the movement on your first tries, so be more attentive in keeping your lower back safe. You can do the low lunge twist to minimize the risk of an injury by limiting the twist to your rib cage while keeping the belly button up. Ensure that your chin is lightly tucked as you reach the top of your head. Go back to your starting pose with your hands down. Step forward and carefully roll-up.

2. Toe Stand or Padangusthasana

This yoga pose, typically performed in Bikram yoga, helps open the hips and strengthen the core of your feet. Warm-up first by doing hip stretches. Be careful if you have a knee problem. Stand on your right leg as your starting pose. Do a half-lotus tree pose by moving the top of your left foot to your right hip. Breathe deeply while ensuring to keep your balance. Carefully bend your right knee as you keep the left foot on top of the left thigh. As you do this, start lifting your right heel until you are up on the ball of your right foot as you squat. Keep your right heel at the center of your body while on a squat.

Extend your fingertips on the floor to get more balance. Lift a hand or both hands, if you can, while keeping your belly firm. Move your hands at the front of your chest in an Anjali mudra pose. Breathe deeply for five counts. Gently go back to your starting pose, breathe deeply, shake both legs, and repeat the sequence on the other side.

3. Deep Side Lunge or Skandasana

There are many ways to execute this yoga pose, depending on where you are most comfortable. You can do this with one foot hooked at the back of your head as you perform a seated forward bend. You can also do this while standing, with one foot, hooked at the back of your head. The pose strengthens the hips and hamstrings and helps in improving your balance and core strength.

Begin with the wide-legged forward bend pose. Bend your knee until you are on a half squat. Keep your right leg straight as you extend your foot and lift your toes from the floor. Rest your weight on your right heel. If you are still finding it difficult to keep your balance, you can opt to keep your hands on the floor. Once you have perfected the movements and balance, you can bend your elbows as you put your hands together in an Anjali mudra pose while keeping your left elbow tucked at the inner part of the left knee. To release the pose, drop your hands to the floor to get support. Breathe deeply before shifting and doing the sequence on the other side.

CHAPTER 4

HOW TO INCORPORATE HYGGE IN YOUR DAILY LIFE

Hygge is a mindset more than anything. It is not mainly about material things but also about what you do to imbibe coziness, warmth, comfort, and love. You may sometimes buy stuff, such as nice blankets and pillows, candles or incense, essential oil, and your favorite food, but all these are not enough to go hyggelige.

Here are the most basic techniques to follow if you intend to embrace the hygge lifestyle:

1. Slow down

You have to find a work-life balance, which means that you don't forget about slowing down even when things at work are too hectic, or there's a pile-up of orders. You have to find ways to become productive without harming your health in the process. Slowing down is a simple investment you do for your general well-being. It allows you to enjoy your space and the people you are with. You work hard for most of your days, but make sure that you don't forget the "me" or "hygge" time wherein you will do whatever feels pleasing and cozy and spend time with your loved ones.

2. Simplicity is favored

What captures the interest of many people about hygge is its simplicity. Many homes and spaces from around the globe have adopted the Scandi décor, which remains a trend up to this day. The main reason for this is the style's simplicity. Hygge promotes contentment and the use of minimal things in decorating, crafting, cooking, or baking. It is more of utilizing what you already have to make your life more pleasant, happier, and contented.

3. Connect with people

Small gatherings with meaningful conversations are important in Danish culture. If you intend to go hygge, you have to make time to meet people, especially those you care about. Dine with them, talk to them in person, or do activities you will all enjoy. It teaches you to speak to your loved ones and listen to them. This is so simple, yet many people tend to disregard it as they go about their busy schedules.

There are many ways to go hygge in every aspect of your life. You can do something hyggelige for your home, clothing, holidays, attitude, and food and drinks.

The Hygge Essentials

The things you'll use to make the experience more hyggelige will depend on your preferences – what makes you happy, what things remind you of your favorite memories, what makes you feel at home. To begin with, you may want to include the things many Danes use in following the hygge lifestyle. Stock and keep these things handy so that you can pull them out and use them whenever you feel the need to slow down and go hygge:

- Candles
- Essential oils
- Blankets and cushions

Candles

Candles are a must-have in hygge. The Danes use them to make their homes feel warm and relaxing. Lighting is something that they seem to be obsessed with due to the fact that they don't get as much natural light in Denmark during winter.

Instead of feeling down in the absence of natural light, Danes found a way to make their winters bearable and cozy by using candles. The light coming from candles bring about comfort since they are not too bright.

The Danes call candles levende lys, which means living light. If you don't have any other props, you can start with candles and use them more often instead of electric light. Artificial and electric lights are not hygge because they are bright and do not feel cozy. If you find candles to be too dim, you can adjust the brightness by lighting more candles. You can have several candles grouped in every room or the preferred corners of your home.

You can look at various physical and online stores for hygge candles. They typically look simple and minimalist in natural colors and with Scandinavian design. They do not have strong scents, just enough to make you feel relaxed without causing headaches.

Make Your Own Candles

The process of creation is hyggelige. You will enjoy the outcome, even more, when you participated in its creation.

The best choice of materials in making candles is all-natural. As a beginner, you can use soy wax that comes from the hydrogenated form of soybean oil. This wax is softer and has a lower temperature than paraffin wax. The wax's melting point depends on the additives; it can range from 120 to 180 degrees.

You can buy soy wax in pellet or flake forms. You can turn them into votive or pillar candles, but they are mostly used in making candles in containers due to the wax's lower melting temperature. In the candle making industry, soy wax is used as straight, combined with other waxes, such as paraffin, palm wax, or beeswax, or mixed with natural oils. You can also add color pigments, but since you want to attain the hygge atmosphere, you can leave the candles in their natural color or use colors with natural and light hues.

Soy wax, aside from being natural, is free from herbicides and pesticides. Candles made from soy can hold the fragrance as they burn. They also burn cleaner than the candles made from paraffin. Even without adding colors, soy candles look nice with off-white or creamy color and a smooth finish. You can use natural dyes if you want to add colors to your candles. Use natural wicks because they will burn efficiently in these candles.

Soy wax is eco-friendly, and it is not expensive. The candles will burn slowly and clean as long as they are well-made.

The best alternative for soy wax is beeswax, which existed long before the introduction of soy. The wax comes from the refined and cleaned wax of the beehives. It burns cleanly like soy wax and biodegradable as well. What makes it better than soy wax is that beeswax is harder and has a longer shelf life.

In making hygge candles, though, soy wax is more preferred since beeswax is more expensive, and it doesn't hold scents for too long due to its distinctive honey scent. The colors of the beeswax candle usually come out as gold or brown.

The Tools You Need

While this will only be a hobby, a pastime you will do when you want to relax or slow down, it is best that you do it right. Since you will need many candles in following the hygge lifestyle, buying the required tools is like an investment. To make it more hyggelige, you can turn the candle making process into a bonding activity you will do with your family or friends.

Here are the needed materials in making soy wax candles:

1. Soy wax. You will add other wax into it depending on what type of candles you're making. You will need pillar candles to make candles that can stand and container wax if you create candles placed in a jar or tin.

2. Color. If you want to add colors to your candles, you can use blocks or liquid dye and dye chips and use a dropper to dispense them.

3. Fragrance oil. This is the last to be added in candle making. This way, the scents won't get cooked out

early in the process. Choose the kinds of scents that feel homey and soothing, as well as fragrances that will remind you of certain seasons and holidays.

4. Wick. Buy a good quality wick with the right size, or else your candle will have poor lighting. Remember that the bigger the number of the wick's size, the larger it is. It is recommended to buy a pre-waxed wire wick and tab to make candle assembly easier, especially in the beginning.

5. Molds and containers. Candle tins are manageable and preferred by the novices in the craft. You can also use small glass jars. For free-standing pillars, you will need a seamless mold. You can also recycle used jars from old candles and canning jars.

6. Thermometer. You can use a candy thermometer if you have one. If not, but the type intended for candle making. Clean it off by wiping it with a piece of cloth while the wax is still warm.

A thermometer is crucial in the process because you have to monitor the wax and make sure it won't overheat. Most waxes available include temperature guidelines in the packaging. For household waxes, the specific melting point is 130 degrees.

· · ·

7. Scale. You will need this for both the wax and the fragrance. You don't have to get the expensive type as long as it can give accurate measurements.

8. Pouring pots and saucepans. If you're going to use pots you already have at home, make sure that you won't use them for anything other purposes than making candles. Use pots that are easy to wipe, made from stainless steel, and has a pouring spout. You will need two saucepans that differ in size to melt the wax using the double boiler method.

9. Labels. Ensure that all your materials for candle making have the corresponding labels. Aside from remembering which is which, you will also have a guide about the temperature setting and melting points of the waxes.

10. Double boiler. You cannot melt wax in direct heat because it can cause a fire. The double boiler method is the safer choice, as long as you only use the material for the craft and not for cooking your food.

11. Workplace. It is not recommended to use your kitchen for candle making. Find a space or room in the house you will designate for the task. You can easily control the people coming into the room. It will

also help to keep a baking soda handy because it serves as a good fire extinguisher.

12. Other supplies. You will need disposable latex gloves for your hands, a small calculator, rubbing alcohol for cleaning the pots, paper towels, and newspaper to protect the space from spillage.

The Candle Making Process

Before starting, make sure that you have gathered all the materials you need. Wipe the containers clean if you're going to use them and anchor a piece of wick in every container. Line up the containers with the wicks near the stove so you can easily access them when it's time to pour the melted wax.

Container Candles

Here are the steps in making container candles:

1. You will need soy wax flakes; take note that each votive-sized candle requires 2 ounces, candle dyes if you intend to add color and scented oils. You can also make unscented candles, but for the purpose of going hygge, scents are essential in helping you relax and feel at ease.

2. Put the wax flakes in the pot placed in a double boiler over a medium-high flame. Stir every once in a

while until completely melted. You will know that the melted wax is pourable when it looks clear. Add a few drops of the scent before the wax turns opaque. When the melted wax changed its color into opaque, it is getting hard, and you will need to reheat it.

3. Pour the wax into your prepared containers while it is hot. Arrange the wicks to ensure that they will remain in the middle of each candle as it hardens. Leave the candles for up to 4 hours or until completely set.

4. Trim the wicks and leave the candles overnight before using them.

Pure Soy Votive Candles

To serve as your guide, you will need 2 ounces of soybean wax for each piece of soy votive candle.

1. Melt wax in the double broiler. Clip the thermometer at the side of the pot to monitor the temperature of the wax. Once melted, it has to be between 170 to 180 degrees. Once it has reached the ideal temperature, add the dye if using, and stir until incorporated. You will need to add a UV inhibitor to the mixture if the candles would get exposed to UV light, such as fluorescent or the sun. Stir for a couple of minutes once you are done adding the dye.

. . .

2. Once the temperature reaches 175 degrees, you can add 1.5 ounces of fragrance oil for every pound of wax. Stir well while monitoring that the temperature won't exceed 200 degrees.

3. Put the molds in a heated oven for 15 minutes before pouring the wax. Arrange them on a flat level surface when ready to use. Heat a pour pot before using it to fill each mold with melted wax up to the brim.

4. Wait until a thin skin begins to form on top of each candle before inserting the wick. Hold the wick at its tip and push it through the thin skin layer until it reaches the bottom of the mold. Make sure that the wick remains straight and placed in the middle of each candle. You have to do this fast, or else holes will form beside the wicks.

5. Leave the candles to set for 5 hours, and cure them for two days before fitting them to holders and using the candles.

The Fragrances

You have two options when it comes to the fragrances used in your candles – fragrance oils or essential oils.

Fragrance oils are synthetic but have the scents of natural plants or flowers, depending on the flavor. They are often referred to as aromatherapy scents, but they lack the essential oils' therapeutic and medicinal elements. They are also cheaper and come in any scents that can be synthetically duplicated. These oils differ in grades based on concentration.

Essential oils are natural and sourced through various plants that have undergone processes, such as cold press or distillation. These oils are used for their aromatic scent and healing characteristics and beauty, bath, and body products. They are more expensive than fragrance oils, and it is important to note that they don't react well to heat. You can still use them in your candles if you intend to go all-natural, but make sure that you don't use dyes either. For candles, choose essential oils with strong scents, such as patchouli, lemongrass, and lavender.

No matter what you choose, use the oils based on the safe levels depending on the amount of wax used. It is also not advisable to use perfumes in candles because most of these products contain alcohol.

The following are the scents typically used in making soy wax candles:

- Apple harvest

- Peach nectar
- Orange chili pepper
- Grapefruit mangosteen
- Citron and mandarin
- Coriander and Tonka
- Sunwashed linen
- Coffee
- Very vanilla
- Chili pepper
- Apple pie
- Black coffee
- Fresh linen
- Frankincense
- Lemongrass
- Lemon
- Chocolate
- Cherry almond
- Cinnamon
- Lime
- Lilac ocean
- Raspberry
- Strawberry
- Sugar cookie
- Dewdrop
- Love spell
- White cake

Essential Oils

Essential oils, despite the name, are not oils since they don't contain fatty acids. They are derived from highly concentrated plants, hence, their medicinal and cosmetic benefits. Your skin easily absorbs these oils, which healing properties include antiviral, anti-fungal, and antibacterial. You must use them with care and according to product safety regulations to ensure you won't have any problems with them.

Here are the most prevalent applications where essential oils are used:

1. Inhalation

You can either do this traditionally or by using a diffuser by adding several oil drops in the tools you'd use for this purpose. Traditionally, you need to put hot water in any container, add the oils, and inhale the vapor. For the diffuser, you will also add water and drops of the oil, which varies depending on the size and type of the product. These days, the most commonly available diffusers in the market include electric heat, cool air nebulizer, candle diffusers, and humidifiers.

2. Compresses

You can use the oils for both hot and cold compresses, typically applied for wounds and bruises, muscle aches, abdominal pain, and skin problems. You need to add 10 drops of the oil to 4 ounces of hot or cold water. Soak a soft cloth to the solution before wrapping it in the affected area. Soak it again once you no longer feel the coldness or warmth. Do this for several minutes or until the discomfort eases.

3. Facial steam

Boil a pot of water and add 5 drops of the essential oil. Cover your head with a towel before placing it above the steam. This practice has been done by the older generations in treating sinuses, migraines, and certain skin problems.

4. Baths

It's best to use a mild oil for this purpose. Add 5 to 10 drops of oil in the water at least 15 minutes before you soak in. This will give enough time for the oil to disperse before you come into the water.

5. Massages

For massages, either you'll do it by yourself or have it done by a professional, use the oils diluted from 2 to 10 percent.

Top Facts about Essential Oils

Here are some facts that you need to know about essential oils before using them:

- When you buy essential oils, read the labels to ensure that they are pure and don't contain perfume or fragrance. They would lose their natural healing properties if additives were used. You can also test the pureness of the oil by putting a drop on a piece of construction paper. You have a pure essential oil if it evaporates fast without leaving noticeable traces. The opposite result means that it may have been diluted with other oils.

- Always use these oils with caution, and take note that they are concentrated. This means that most of them can be harmful when undiluted and used directly on the skin. You have to combine them with carrier oils or dilute them with alcohol, waxes, or butter. If the label says that the oil is safe to use even when undiluted, use it sparingly and never apply too much of it on your skin.

Some of the oils are typically safe to use on the skin even when undiluted, including German chamomile, rose geranium, lavender, sandalwood, and tea tree. If you use the oils on your children's skin, always dilute even the types said to be safe on the skin when undiluted. Children have thinner skin than adults, so they are more delicate and prone to skin reactions.

- Perform a skin patch test first before using the essential oils, undiluted or not, on your skin. Add a drop of the oil to half a teaspoon of carrier oil, such as jojoba, sweet almond, or olive oil. Mix well, rub on the inside part of your arm, and leave for a few hours. It is safe if you did not develop any allergic reactions, such as swelling or itchiness. Wash the skin area at once you notice any redness, and make sure that you have gotten rid of all the oil.
- Many of these oils can be taken internally and not recommended to be used by pregnant women.
- The oils' shelf life ranges from 5 up to 10 years, except for citrus oils that will last for a year or two.
- Store the oils properly by keeping them in their original dark bottle containers. Place the bottles in a warm and dry place, and keep them out of direct sunlight.

Hygge and Aromatherapy

The hygge atmosphere wouldn't be complete without aromatherapy. Aside from having scented candles (which you can do on your own), you can use essential oils in many ways to diffuse their scent into your space. If you don't have a diffuser or sprayer, you can add a couple of drops of your chosen oil to a cotton ball and leave it in a corner or at your bedside table. The scent will waft through the air as the oil evaporates from the cotton.

Use the right blends of essential oils and carrier oils to suit your mood and help you relax and get cozy. Here are some blends you can diffuse or place in a cotton ball for an hyggelige aromatherapy experience using essential oils.

Summer Blends

- 2 drops of rosemary essential oil
- 4 drops of grapefruit essential oil
- 3 drops of peppermint essential oil

Thanksgiving Blend

- 3 drops of sweet orange essential oil
- 2 drops of clove essential oil
- 3 drops of cinnamon essential oil

Cuddle Blend

- 3 drops of sweet orange essential oil
- 3 drops of frankincense essential oil
- 2 drops of vetiver essential oil
- 3 drops of cinnamon essential oil

Scent of Autumn

- 1 drop of cinnamon essential oil
- 2 drops of ginger essential oil
- 2 drops of sweet orange essential oil

Holiday Blend

- 1 drop of juniper essential oil
- 1 drop of cinnamon essential oil
- 1 drop of clove essential oil
- 1 drop of orange essential oil
- 1 drop of pine essential oil

Winter Scent

- 1 drop of eucalyptus essential oil
- 1 drop of pine essential oil

- 2 drops of cedarwood essential oil

Slumber Time

- 1 drop vetiver
- 4 drops lavender

Perfect Spring

- 4 drops of lemon essential oil
- 3 drops of clary sage essential oil
- 2 drop of ylang-ylang essential oil

Winter Blend

- 3 drops of balsam fir essential oil
- 3 drops of pine essential oil
- 3 drops of bergamot essential oil
- 3 drops of frankincense essential oil

Meditation Blend

- 4 drops of frankincense essential oil

- 2 drops of patchouli essential oil
- 2 drops of sandalwood essential oil

Clear Mind Scent

- 3 drops of mandarin essential oil
- 2 drops of rosemary essential oil
- 2 drops of vetiver essential oil
- 3 drops of frankincense essential oil

Serenity

- 2 drops of patchouli essential oil
- 4 drops of frankincense essential oil
- 3 drops of bergamot essential oil

Uplifting Scent

- 3 drops of bergamot essential oil
- 2 drops of ylang-ylang essential oil
- 3 drops of lavender essential oil

~

The Essential Oils

Here are some useful information about the most commonly used essential oils in a hyggelige aromatherapy:

1. Orange essential oil (Citrus sinensis)

The oil comes from the peels of the fruit, derived through cold compression. It has anti-inflammatory, antidepressant, and antiseptic properties. The scent can help in dealing with sexual dysfunction and in getting rid of body toxins.

If you ingested this bitter-tasting oil in large quantities, you might experience loss of appetite, vomiting, and nausea. The oil blends well with other oils, such as black pepper, clove, ginger, and vetiver.

2. Ginger essential oil (Zingiber Officinale)

The oil comes from the roots of this herb commonly used as a spice. It heals body pains, spasms, and wounds. It helps bring back your skin color, improve brain and memory functions, and benefit the stomach.

Use this strong oil sparingly. It combines well with other oils, such as rosewood, lemon, orange, and ylang-ylang.

3. Cinnamon essential oil (Cinnamomum zeylanicum)

This oil is popularly used in traditional medicines, such as the Ayurveda in India. It has antimicro-bial and astringent properties, is used as a brain tonic, and can treat respiratory problems, bad breath, breastfeeding issues, diabetes, and colon cancer.

It has to be always diluted and never taken inter-nally. It blends well with other oils, such as lavender, geranium, lemon, and cardamom.

4. Pine essential oil (Pinus slvestris)

The needles and fresh twigs of the pine tree go through steam distillation to extract the oil. It can deal with skin problems, stress disorder, body pains, slow metabolism, urinary tract infection, mental fatigue, and respiratory ailment. This is considered one of the most important oils in aromatherapy. It blends well with sage, rosemary, and cedarwood.

5. Clove essential oil (Syzgium aromaticum)

The oil comes from the flower bud of the clove. It is used in dental care, such as treating cavities and toothache. It also deals with stress, indigestion, skin-care, blood circulation and purification, diabetes, cholera, sties, low immune system, and premature ejaculation. It is strong, so the oil has to be diluted before using. You can blend it with grapefruit, rose-mary, cinnamon, lemon, nutmeg, and basil.

· · ·

6. Cedarwood essential oil (Cedrus atlantica)

The oil comes from the wood of the tree, derived through steam distillation. It helps in treating wounds, contracting muscles and gums, and boosting blood circulation. It can also calm the nerves and can aid in treating colds and flu. It is also used as an insecticide. The oil is highly potent and, if taken internally, may lead to nausea, vomiting, and damages to the digestive system. Use this oil in small doses, and you can mix it with bergamot, neroli, lemon, jasmine, or cypress.

7. Eucalyptus essential oil (Eucalyptus Globulus)

The oil comes from the fresh leaves of the ever-green eucalyptus tree. It has decongestant, antiseptic, and antibacterial properties. It can help treat respira-tory problems, wounds, muscle pains, certain skin problems, mental exhaustion, fever, intestinal germs, and diabetes. It is advised to seek your doctor's approval before using the oil if you are undergoing homeopathic treatments. It blends well with thyme, rosemary, lavender, and frankincense.

8. Lavender essential oil (Lavandula angustifolia)

The flower of the plant is mostly used to derive the oil through steam distillation. The oil is popular in aromatherapy and perfumery. It is both soothing and relaxing and can treat skin inflammation, headaches, body pains, dermatitis, sunburn, burns, and insect bites. Pregnant women and those with diabetes are advised to refrain from using this oil. It blends well with clary sage, pine, nutmeg, cedarwood, and geranium.

9. Ylang Ylang essential oil (Cananga odorata)

The oil comes from the fresh flowers of the plant, derived through steam distillation. The oil is effective in dealing with low sexual libido, depression, nervous problems, and inflammation. It is also good for the stomach and colon. The oil is non-toxic but still has to be used in low dosages. It blends well with other oils, such as grapefruit, lavender, and bergamot.

10. Clary Sage essential oil (Salvia sclarea)

The oil is obtained from the buds and leaves of the herb through steam distillation. The herb is widely used in keeping the eye healthy. The oil, on the other hand, can balance nervous functions and works as an antidepressant. It kills bacteria and makes wounds heal faster.

The oil is obtained from the buds and leaves of the plant through the process of steam distillation. Clary sage is an herb popular for its medicinal benefits, especially for eye health. The oil is used to deal with convulsions, spasms, low sexual libido, and high blood pressure. It is also generally good for the stomach and uterus.

The oil is slightly expensive than the other essential oils and must never be used in high dosages. It blends well with lavender, pine, jasmine, lime, lemon, sandalwood, and geranium.

11. Lemon essential oil (Citrus limonum)

The oil, which smells fresh and sharp, has antiseptic properties. It is used in healing wounds and preventing bacterial growth. It is good for the gums and skin and is used in dealing with health issues, such as fever, hemorrhage, and hair loss. It blends well with oils, such as tea tree, ylang-ylang, geranium, rose, and lavender.

12. Grapefruit essential oil (Citrus Paradisi)

The oil is extracted from the peel of the fruit through compression. It helps in fighting depression, infections, and treating wounds faster. It is recommended to wait and allow the skin to completely absorb the oil before exposing yourself to the sun to avoid suffering from skin irritation. It blends well with frankincense, geranium, lavender, and bergamot.

13. Frankincense essential oil (Boswellia Carteri)

The oil is widely used in religious customs and

rites, and it is also popular in the cosmetics industry. It has antiseptic and disinfectant properties. It promotes healthy cell regeneration, aids in digestion, inflammation, anxiety, and treats colds and coughs. It is also used in making wounds and scars heal faster. Pregnant women cannot use it due to the oil's astringent properties. It blends well with myrrh, lavender, orange, lime, bergamot, benzoin, and pine.

14. Bergamot essential oil (Citrus bergamia)

The oil is obtained from the rind of the fruit through cold compression. It is commonly included in regular black tea. The oil's strong scent makes it popular in the perfume industry. It has digestive, antibiotic, antidepressant, and disinfectant properties. It can cure pain, spasms, mood swings, and body odor. The oil has bergapten, which makes it poisonous when exposed to the sun. It blends well with other citrus oils, as well as with ylang-ylang, clary sage, black pepper, nutmeg, and rosemary.

15. Mandarin essential oil
   (Citrus reticulata)

The oil is obtained from the fresh peels of the fruit through cold compression. It has antiseptic and antispasmodic properties. It is used in boosting blood flow, lymph circulation, blood purification, and cell regeneration. It also makes the body toned and is generally good for the stomach. Some people develop an allergic reaction to the oil due to its phototoxicity. It blends well with lemon, clove, bergamot, lavender, nutmeg, lime, and orange.

≈

Blankets and Cushions

The Danes need blankets in hygge because of the cold winters. They typically use the kinds made of wool or fleece to give them a feeling of snuggling. You can also use blankets if you want to feel cozy even when the weather is not freezing; just make sure that you use the kind made from lighter materials, such as cotton. On the other hand, cushions, no matter what their sizes are, provide comfort, and you can use them as a cuddle or while you are reading a book.

≈

Other Hygge Essentials

Here are some more items you can include in your hygge kit:

- A journal or diary
- Hand cream and body lotion
- Fragrant bath soap
- A box you'd fill with the list of things you are grateful for
- Warm socks
- Face mask

- Chocolates
- A list of your friends and family's contact information
- Magazines and books
- Pen and notebooks
- Letters from loved ones
- Postcards
- Photo album

CHAPTER 5

THE OTHER ASPECTS OF HYGGE: HOME, CLOTHING, BUDGETING, AND THE HOLIDAYS

Hygge is a minimalist lifestyle, making it hard for those who have gotten used to acquiring material possessions. It may take getting used to, but all your efforts will be beneficial in the long run.

Hygge and Your Home

Home décor the hygge way means creating a warm and safe space for your loved ones. It's important to keep things simple by keeping in mind the following tips:

1. You have to create an atmosphere that feels homey and comfortable

Choose the areas you'd use for snuggling and cozying up. Fill these areas with a soft comforter and fluffy pillows. Besides the space near the fireplace, you can also create nooks on a love seat or window bench. Pick the spots you'd have a good time enjoying your peace, having a cup of hot coffee or cocoa, or reading a good book.

No-no's: Do not make a space with limited seating and avoid using modern-looking furniture pieces. You are not aiming for extravagance, but simplicity and comfort.

2. Choose a neutral color scheme for the paint and things you add to your home

Your space's overall theme must be relaxing, so it is best to stick to a neutral color palette. You can add things and decors in pastel colors, such as hues of cream, brown, and gray. Whatever color you choose, make sure that it is not too bright and overwhelming.

No-no's: Do not put anything inside your home that looks too distracting and overly bright.

3. Add texture

A minimalist home will look more interesting when you add texture by using the right decorations. You can use materials made of wool or wood, and add flowers with similar colors and other things that will make your space more appealing but still relaxing.

No-no's: Avoid getting anything that will disrupt the aesthetics with textures and colors that do not match the house's overall theme.

. . .

4. Use candles as decors throughout your home

Candles are relaxing, calming, and romantic, which make them hygge-perfect. You can use them to provide warm lights to your space. You can also make your own candles and enjoy every step of the process.

No-no's: Do not use candles with bright colors and emit strong scents.

5. Light your fireplace

Use your fireplace, if you have one, to make the ambiance warm and cozy. You can gather your family and friends around the fire to bond and spend quality time with. Huddling around the fireplace is frequently done by the Danes. If you don't have a fireplace, you can use candles instead to give out the same vibe, or you can also make a bonfire outside.

No-no's: Do not treat the fireplace as a decoration. If you have one, make sure that you use it.

6. Bring in a cheery atmosphere by using twinkly lights

Choose the lights with soft and pleasant colors. You can use them to add a festive vibe to your home so that it will look homey and happy at the same time. You can place them in the outdoor patio, living room, or bedroom. They don't look overwhelming but give out a similar appeal to candles.

No-no's: Avoid using bright and bulky lamps with distracting glow or too bright lights.

7. Turn your bathroom into a relaxing retreat space

Take inspiration from spas when arranging your bathroom. Make this space something peaceful, pleasant, and a go-to area when you need rejuvenation and rest. Install enough storage spaces and look for the kinds that do not consume too much space. Make the area neat, light candles, and use soft towels and comfy robes.

No-no's: Stop using your bathroom as a mere utility, and start using the space to promote hygge.

Hygge and Clothing

Hygge is all about comfort when it comes to clothing. The style and materials will depend on the season and weather. The Danes follow a styling called top bulky, which means layering, plenty of black, woolen socks, and scarf.

Hygge Clothing During Winter

Here are some tips on how to dress up when the weather is cold:

1. Bulk up your wardrobe with oversized sweaters. The key here is to buy one size larger than your usual size.

2. Think about warmth and comfort when choosing what cardigan to wear or which pair of wool socks you will use for the day.

3. Relaxed pants, like yoga pants and sweatpants, will go well with puffer jackets. If you decide to stay at home all day, you can settle with a thick but comfy robe and pajamas.

4. The Danish people love wearing black no matter what the season is. If you'd rather tone down the black in your repertoire, you can settle with navy, brown, or muted gray clothing or accents. You have to choose accents that are not too loud or bright. Use them sparingly if you feel like you must.

5. Minimalism is quite important in hygge in all aspects, including fashion. You can try to insert a slight individualism through structuring, wearing a white pump or beanie, or having piercings.

6. Instead of using a bulky scarf, you can settle for the quilted type that matches your overall outfit. If a

scarf is not your thing, you will look hygge fashion-friendly with a sweater tied around your neck.

7. Master the practice of layering, whether you will stay indoors or go outdoors. Inside your home, you can sport a layering comprised of leggings, socks, pants, bomber, and sweatshirt. If going out, you can try a midi dress, blouse, and ivory leggings. The hygge fashion doesn't have a rule as long as you feel warm and have enough protection to survive the cold weather.

8. While staying at home during the cold season, you can use the time to take pictures with your outfit complementing your background. Wear clothes in colors that match your house and accents.

Hygge Clothing During Spring and Summer

Coziness doesn't have to end as the season changes. The hygge trend in fashion pertains more to furs, ripped denim, thick socks, oversized knitwear worn over your newly bleached hair on a messy bun. Once the season changes, you only have to make some alterations to don fashion that fit the hygge lifestyle and doesn't compromise your comfort.

Here are some tips on what to wear during spring and summer:

1. Crochet, feathers, and furs

While furs may be out of season in terms of clothing, such as coats, you can use them as an element or accent. You can carry a small fur bag or use fur or feather as a bag accessory. You can use crochet details on your pants or tops. You can also wear accessories with crocheted items, even feathers, and furs. Whites and earth tones are still your best choices for summer and spring when it comes to fashion. You will never go wrong with colors, such as pink, beige, and grey.

2. Look for the best alternatives for your oversized knits

While oversize knitwear defines hyggelige during winter, it no longer fits the weather during spring or summer. You can wear light knitwear as long as it feels comfy. You can also look for summer dresses that look oversized. Refrain from wearing body-hugging materials made from thick fabrics. You can also don off-shoulder tops to give off the perfect spring or summer vibe.

3. Happy footwear

The season calls for something fun, like ruffles and bows, on your footwear. You can wear velvet mules with bows or comfy sandals with ruffles as the highlight.

∾

Hygge on a Budgeting

One of the most important factors why many people are interested in the hygge lifestyle is the cost. It is more of going back to the basics concept and will only cost a little. It is something that anyone can try since the changes focus more on behavior than the things to buy. While it worked for the Danes, it will take great effort for people who have been consumed by their hectic schedules for a long time. They have gotten used to working non-stop, not realizing until it's too late that they have sacrificed their personal enjoyment and relationships.

This is where hygge can help – it makes you realize what you have been missing, what you are depriving yourself of. It doesn't stop you from working hard, but it reminds you that as a human being, your health will eventually suffer if you will continue with the "all work no play" kind of lifestyle.

Hygge prompts you to take a breather every once in a while and surround yourself with things and people that make you feel comfortable and loved. It also focuses on the activities that you will enjoy but won't break the bank.

As hygge continues to capture many people's attention worldwide, there are trends in hygge products being made available with hefty price tags. Everything you'll need to shift into the lifestyle can easily be bought at various stores – yoga retreats, skincare products, sewing patterns and materials, relaxing wallpaper and paints, vegan shepherd's pie, cashmere cardigans, and more.

THE OTHER ASPECTS OF HYGGE: HOME, CLOT... 91

Do not feel bad if you can't afford these products. You can start your hygge journey without them and instead, focus on the more important aspects of the lifestyle – make time for your loved ones, embrace nature, and slow down.

Here are some hygge ideas that won't cost you a fortune, perfect for those interested to take the shift but are still tight on a budget:

1. Wear something comfortable

If you work in an office with a strict formal rule for the attire, reward yourself with the thought of coming home at the end of each day to wear anything you want and any clothing item that makes up for hours in the office when it feels stiff and serious. Go completely hygge with your clothes when you are at home. Wear the classic hygge staples, such as knitted socks and a heavy sweater when the weather is cold. You can wear anything you want that makes you breathe, clothes that will make it easier for you to sleep soundly once you hit the bed.

2. Walk outside

Most people tied up with their busy schedules often walk alone out of frustration or whenever they feel like they can no longer control the situation, and they need time off. It is the same with hygge, but you will do it consciously, and most of the time, you'd ask companions to walk with you. The Danish people love walking in all kinds of weather, yes, including rainy days and wintertime. You can do it as an exercise, like walking on your own in the morning or walking your dog around the neighborhood. To make it more hyggelige, you can schedule walks with your friends or loved ones. Take this chance to catch up and talk about anything under the sun. Walking is good for your health, and it will not cost you a cent.

3. Share your food

Hygge gives you a chance to let your inner chef comes out. It is more about enjoying the process of food preparation and sharing the dishes with your loved ones. You don't have to prepare anything fancy. Hygge is not about haute cuisine, but more about comfort food. You also don't have to do any fancy preparation. It is even okay to be messy for as long as you find the process enjoyable. You can always ask for help to clean the mess once the food is done.

Comfort food varies from person to person. You may have your favorites, like your grandmother's recipe of a cabbage or pumpkin soup or the fudgiest brownie only your father can prepare. For the Danes, some of their favorite comfort foods include rich cakes, meatballs, anything potato, and pancakes. When you invite friends over to your house, you can hold a potluck and ask everybody to bring dishes you can enjoy together. This will save you more money without limiting the fun you'll have in the company of your guests.

· · ·

4. Enjoy hot drinks

You can enjoy a hot drink during your break time at work or whenever you want to enjoy the cold or wet weather. It looks and feels cozy to hold a steaming hot drink in your hand while sitting comfortably or sharing the experience with a friend or loved one. You can drink hot chocolate, tea, or coffee. You can also try Denmark's ultimate hygge drink, the spiced mulled wine they refer to as glogg. This brings you back to the basics of enjoying the drinks you can easily prepare at home without the need to spend a fortune on expensive coffee shops. You can always try to copy the recipes of your favorite expensive drinks, but it will still be cheaper when you make them yourself.

5. Light candles

Danish people use the term "lyselukker" to refer to people they consider as a spoilsport or the kind of person who "puts out the candles." This is how much they are obsessed with candles, which comprise the top list of the ways to go hygge. Candles are not that expensive but make sure you get them from reliable sources, and the labels state what they are made of. You can also try making your own candles to get more savings while learning some-thing new and enjoying the process. Candles may help a lot in turning an ambiance into something relaxing and comforting but always use them respon-sibly. Place lighted candles in areas out of reach of small children and pets. It is also important to put off the fire when you leave the house to prevent accidents.

6. Enjoy riding the bike

Biking is quite popular in Denmark that Copenhagen, its capital city, was given recognition as the first official Bike City in the world. What makes this activity hygge is that it moves slower than cars, so you will have time to enjoy the view. This is also a good form of exercise, and studies show that people who ride their bikes to work are happier and healthier than those who don't. You can always choose to buy second-hand bikes if you don't have one. It's not important how much is the bike you are using but how much you enjoy and benefit from it.

7. Light a fire

Watching the flames coming from a fireplace and other sources of fire is another favorite hygge activity. It is more relaxing than watching the candle burning. During the winter season, it feels good to watch the flame and hear the crackling fire coming from an indoor fireplace. It's not a problem if you don't have one; you can stream a video on your television of fire, complete with good visuals and sound effects. You can gather around the screen and light candles nearby. During summer, you can create an outdoor fire pit where you will gather your loved ones for a picnic, barbecue, or meaningful conversations.

8. Take the time to read

Reading a printed book feels therapeutic for many enthusiasts. Aside from the content, the activity is a good way to relax and detach yourself from work and your social media sites, even for a time. You can do it anywhere you please, as long as you feel comfortable, nice, and warm.

9. Play board games with your family or friends

Board games bring back the feeling of having fun without spending a lot or doing what you love to do when you were young. You can have a gathering at your home void of gadgets. Prepare tabletop games you can enjoy with your companions. It's simple, relaxing, and fun.

10. Watch the television

The Danes love spending hygge time with their companions watching television shows. The top choices include scary but fictional shows and the kind involving killers and police procedures. Anything fictional that give you a good scare or goosebumps is okay in hygge. If you want to relax, though, avoid watching real-life scary happenings in documentaries or news.

. . .

11. Bond over singing

Singing along to songs has been a popular bonding activity in Denmark from the 60s up to now. Most of them have copies of folk songbooks. They enjoy singing different kinds of songs as long as they promote belonging, community, cheerfulness, and simplicity. This bonding activity is fun and won't cost you anything. You can use your favorite songs or ask a family or friend to play an instrument, and everybody will sing along.

12. Cuddle

Snuggling feels good, and it makes you feel loved. You can do it with your kids, best friend, or your partner. You can also cuddle with your pets. It's a simple activity, yet quite comforting and fun.

∾

Hygge and the Holiday Seasons

Holidays can be fun and stressful, and hygge will teach you how to enjoy the holidays with more fun and less stress. Here are some useful tips to make your holiday celebrations hyggeligt:

1. You can break the traditions if you can't keep up with them.

Why would you stress yourself out trying to recreate your grandmother's recipe of a pie when you continually fail no matter what you do? Be easy on yourself and ask a family member or a friend to join you in discovering other recipes you can serve during the holidays. You can always learn the pie recipe when you don't feel any pressure, and you are not obliged to serve it to a group of people.

2. Always remember that there will always be holiday fails. No matter how much effort you put into the gathering, somebody will always have stomach pain, a child will mess the décor, or a turkey will get burnt. Instead of getting disappointed, the least you could do is laugh about the circumstances and add them to your happy memories of the event.

3. Before shopping for a big event, list out all that you need and check the list many times before hitting the road. This way, you will have everything you need when it is time to do the preparations. Do not get frustrated over the presents you were not able to buy.

Hygge is more about the company and not about the material things you give out during the occasion.

4. Be in the moment and celebrate the main reason why you are gathering together. Forget about the negativity you feel over one friend or an age-old family argument. Set those aside and celebrate the event.

5. Remember that you are human and you can't do everything perfectly. Do no sweat the small stuff, such as a dusty baseboard or an unfixed photo frame. Your visitors will not remember those details for as long as you give them a fun and memorable event where everybody feels welcome and happy.

6. If you intend to invite people over to an event for the holidays, make plans and let them know early on about the date. They may have other plans, so you should know beforehand how many of them can come. If other people have better plans and asked you to celebrate with them instead, think about it before refusing. It might be best for everyone to be gathered and celebrate the hygge way.

7. Ask for help from your guests even when you are the host. It is the holiday, and you all deserve to take

a break and enjoy it. It will be better and easier for everybody to join hands in the preparations and to clean up. Do not be afraid to ask, and you will be amazed at how much they want to help.

8. If you have kids and want them to have memorable holidays, think about your childhood. You can repeat the experiences your parents did to make you happy when you were a child. This is also a good way to refresh your memory about the things that can ruin your kids' holiday, so you should refrain from doing them.

9. You don't have to fill the gathering with too many happenings. You can have fewer activities that everybody can participate in and enjoy. You only have to make sure that you have activities and food that your guests of all ages will like. You wouldn't want to be caught looking where you stored the popcorn or candies when some children start getting bored.

10. Enjoy the intimacy of the celebration. You can take as many pictures as you want, but you must not post all of them on your social media sites. It is time to bond with who you are with instead of connecting to the online world.

CHAPTER 6

HYGGE: FOOD AND DRINKS

The Danish culture places importance on their food and how their dishes are prepared and consumed. If you have a gathering coming up, make sure you prepare your place with the right decors. Set the ambiance with enough lighting and suitable music. You can also drape furs over your chairs and have some simple flower arrangements ready. The key here is to turn your place into something cozy that your guests will feel good even though you will only share two or three simple dishes.

You don't have to prepare Danish food for your event to become hygge, but it will not hurt to try. Here are some of the most sumptuous dishes and beverages loved by the Danes, especially when they are celebrating anything the hygge way:

Open-Face Sandwich – Herring Smorrebrod

This is a traditional Danish sandwich, referred to as Smorrebrod, both considered food, and art. Eating the sandwich entails etiquette – it should be eaten in one order. You must consume the herring first, then the other fish, meat, and then cheese in eating the sandwich. You must only eat the sandwich using a fork and a knife but never with your hands. Use rye bread when the ingredients include herring, which you will smear with duck fat or butter before adding the topping. Toast the sandwich frequently so it will taste excellent whenever someone would like to eat.

Serves: 2

Ingredients:

- 1 hardboiled egg (thinly sliced)
- 2 tablespoons red clover sprouts
- 8 fresh cucumber slices (divided)
- 4 teaspoons capers (rinsed and divided)
- 2 sprigs dill (divided)
- 2 sprigs scallions (divided)
- 2 sprigs green onions (divided)
- 1/2 medium shallot (thinly sliced and divided)
- 1 jar marinated Herring fillets (or pickled)
- 5 tablespoons sour cream
- 2 tablespoons olive oil
- 1 teaspoon Dijon mustard
- 1 medium beet (steamed until soft, peeled, and cubed)
- 1 tablespoon butter (divided)

- 2 slices rye bread

Directions:

1. Put olive oil, sour cream, mustard, and beet in a food processor. Process until smooth and creamy, and transfer to a piping bag.

2. Spread butter on each side of the bread slice. Pipe small mounds of the beet mousse in each bread. Place the herring slices and the egg slices. Add the dill, green onion, scallion, shallot, and cucumber slices.

3. Top each bread with 2 teaspoon of capers before serving.

～

Anything Potato

The Dutch loves potatoes and dishes with this vegetable are staples in their hygge gatherings.

Hot Dutch Potato Salad

Ingredients:

- 4 bacon slices (diced)
- 1 teaspoon sugar
- 1 teaspoon salt
- 3 hard-boiled eggs
- 1 egg (beaten)
- 2 1/2 pounds of cooked potatoes (cubed)
- Pepper to taste
- 1/4 cup vinegar
- 1/4 cup raw carrot (grated)
- 1/2 cup green pepper (chopped)
- 1/2 cup onion (minced)

Directions:

1. Cook the diced bacon in a pan over medium flame until crisp. Add the green pepper and onion. Saute for 3 minutes. Place the beaten egg, vinegar, sugar, salt, and pepper. Cook for a minute. Stir in the diced hard-boiled eggs, carrots, and potatoes. Keep stirring until combined.

2. Serve while hot.

Potato Salad Dressing

Ingredients:

- 1 tablespoon flour
- 1/2 cup vinegar
- 1/2 cup sugar
- 1/2 cup water
- 2 tablespoons butter
- 1 egg (beaten)
- 1/4 teaspoon pepper
- 1/2 teaspoon salt

Directions:

1. Put the egg in a bowl. Whisk as you add sugar and flour.

2. Put water in a pan over medium flame, and stir in the egg mixture. Add the following ingredients and stir after each addition: vinegar, butter, salt, and pepper. Stir until thick and bring to a boil.

3. Leave cool before using it as a salad dressing.

Dutch Country Bean Soup

Ingredients:

- 1 pound soup beans (soaked in water overnight)
- 1 can tomato sauce
- Salt and pepper to taste
- 1 cup diced celery
- 1 ham bone
- 2 teaspoons minced parsley
- 1/2 cup diced potatoes
- 1/2 cup chopped onion

Directions:

1. Drain water from the beans before putting them in a pot over a high flame. Add the home bone and freshwater, and cook for 2 hours. Put the potatoes, celery, onion, parsley, and tomato sauce. Season with salt and pepper.

2. Turn heat to low once it boils, and leave to simmer until the veggies are cooked. Transfer the ham bone to a chopping board, and trim the meat, chop, put back to the soup, and discard the bone.

3. You can top the soup with sliced hard-boiled egg before serving.

Corn Chowder

Ingredients:

- 4 bacon slices (diced)
- 1 tablespoon minced celery
- 1 tablespoon pepper
- 4 cups milk
- 2 tablespoons minced onion
- 2 cups corn kernels
- 2 potatoes (diced)
- 3 tomatoes (sliced)
- Salt and pepper to taste

Directions:

1. Cook the diced bacon in the pan over medium flame until browned. Add the celery, onion, and pepper. Continue stirring until the bacon is crisp. Put the corn kernels and leave to cook for 4 minutes. Stir in the tomatoes and potatoes. Season to taste before covering the pan. Leave to simmer for half an hour.

2. Stir in the milk and leave to boil.

3. Add chopped parsley on top of the soup before serving.

Gruumbier Suupe (Potato Soup)

Ingredients:

- 4 cups potatoes (diced)
- 3 tablespoons flour
- Salt and pepper to taste
- 1 egg (beaten)
- 1 onion
- 4 cups milk
- Parsley
- 1 tablespoon butter

Directions:

1. Put enough water in the pot to cover the onion and diced potatoes. Set the flame on medium-high. Bring to a boil, then add milk, and season with salt and pepper. Leave to simmer.

2. Put butter in a saucepan over medium flame and mix until melted. Add flour and stir until browned.

3. Gradually add the flour and butter mixture to the potatoes.

4. Beat the egg and add a bit amount of water. Add to the soup and leave to cook for a couple of minutes. Garnish soup with chopped parsley before serving.

Sweet Potato Croquettes

Ingredients:

- 2 cups mashed sweet potatoes
- Breadcrumbs
- 1 egg white (slightly beaten)
- 1 tablespoon sugar
- 1 tablespoon butter
- 1 teaspoon salt

Directions:

1. Put the mashed sweet potatoes, melted butter, sugar, and salt in a bowl. Mix well. Form patties or croquette rolls from the mixture using your hands. Place in a bowl, cover, and chill for 30 minutes.

2. Roll the croquettes in breadcrumbs. Dip each piece in the beaten egg white and cover with breadcrumbs.

3. Arrange the coated croquettes in a greased baking dish. Bake in a preheated oven at 400 degrees for 20 minutes.

～

Hygge Hot Soup Recipes
Split Pea Soup
Ingredients:

- 1 ham bone
- 1 onion (chopped)
- 1 celery stalk (chopped)
- 1 pound split peas (rinsed and drained)
- Salt and pepper to taste
- 4 cups water
- 2 carrots (sliced)

Directions:

1. Place the peas, ham bone, and veggies in a pot over medium flame. Simmer for 3 hours while stirring every once in a while.

2. Discard the ham bone and put the peas in a coarse sieve. Push the peas back to the pot and season with salt and pepper. Add milk if the soup is too thick to make it thinner.

3. Serve the soup with toasted croutons.

Beef Soup with Dumplings

Ingredients:

- 8 cups water
- 1/2 cup milk
- 1 1/2 cups flour
- 2 pounds stewing beef
- 1 soup bone
- Salt and pepper to taste
- 1 egg

Directions:

1. Put water and the soup bone in a pot over a high flame. Season with salt and pepper, and cook the beef until tender.

2. Discard the soup bone before adding water until the pot has about 8 cups.

3. Prepare the dumplings. Mix the flour and beaten egg in a bowl until thick. Put a spoonful of the batter at a time and drop into the broth. Leave to boil for 4 minutes.

Merry Vegetable Soup

Ingredients:

- Black pepper to taste
- 2 teaspoons salt
- 8 cups water
- 1 cup chopped celery
- 1 cup chopped onion
- 1 cup tomatoes
- 2 pounds stewing beef
- 1 soup bone

Directions:

1. Put water, meat, and soup bone in a pot over a high flame, and leave to boil for 2 hours.

2. Transfer the stewing beef to a chopping board, cut into small pieces, and put them back into the pot. Add the celery, onions, tomatoes, and other vegetables you want to your soup. You can use diced carrots, potatoes, turnip, shredded cabbage, chopped peppers, peas, corn, and string beans. Boil the soup until all the veggies are cooked and tender.

Chicken Corn Soup

Ingredients:

- 1 onion (minced)
- 16 cups water
- 1/2 cup chopped celery
- Salt and pepper to taste
- 2 hard-boiled eggs
- Corn kernels (from 10 ears of corn)
- 1 4-pound stewing hen

For the rivels

- A little amount of milk
- A pinch of salt
- 1 egg
- 1 cup flour

Directions:

1. Boil water in a pot over a high flame as you roughly cut the chicken. Put the meat in the boiling water, and then add the onion and salt. Cook until the meat is tender.

2. Transfer the cooked meat to a chopping board, cut into small pieces, and put them back in the pot. Stir as you add the corn kernels and celery. Season to taste. Simmer over medium flame.

2. Prepare the rivels. Mix all the ingredients in a bowl using a fork or your fingers. Mux until small crumbs are formed. Put the rivels to the soup.

3. Chop the hard-boiled eggs before adding them to the soup. Leave to boil for 15 minutes.

Chicken Noodle Soup
 Ingredients:

- 1 carrot (sliced)
- 1 teaspoon peppercorns
- 1 tablespoon chopped parsley
- 4 pounds stewing chicken (cut into serving sizes)
- 3 cups cooked noodles
- 2 1/2 teaspoons salt
- 10 cups water
- 1 onion (chopped)
- 1 bay leaf
- Salt and pepper to taste

 Directions:
 1. Put water and meat in a pot over a high flame, and leave until it boils. Leave to simmer over medium flame for 3 hours.
 2. Transfer the meat to a chopping board, skim off the fat, and put the meat back in the pot along with the veggies. Season soup with salt and pepper. Add the noodles once it boils and leave simmer for 20 minutes.

Hygge Meat Recipes
Leberknoedel (Liver Noodles)
Ingredients:

- 1 onion (minced)
- 1/2 cup flour
- 1 tablespoon butter
- 2 eggs (beaten)
- 1 pound calf's liver
- Salt and pepper to taste
- 1/4 teaspoon marjoram
- 1/4 teaspoon cloves

Directions:

1. Boil water in a pot and add the meat. Simmer for half an hour over medium flame

2. Transfer the meat to a chopping board, trim off the ligaments and skin from the calf's liver, and grind until fine.

3. Transfer meat to a bowl, and add the beaten eggs, butter, and onion. Mix thoroughly. Gradually add flour as you mix until the paste becomes stiff. Shape small balls from the batter using your hands and put them in the soup. Leave it to simmer for 15 minutes.

Dutch Beef with Onions

Ingredients:

- 2 tablespoons flour
- 2 tablespoons butter
- Salt and pepper to taste
- 1/2 cup meat stock
- 1 tablespoon vinegar
- 1 1/2 pounds beef
- 1 onion (minced)

Directions:

1. Cook meat in a pot with boiling water until tender.

2. Transfer meat to a chopping board and slice it into bite-size pieces.

3. Prepare the onion sauce. Put the butter in a pan over medium flame and stir until melted. Add the minced onion and cook for 3 minutes while constantly stirring. Add flour and mix until browned. Add the meat stock and vinegar, season with salt and pepper, and bring to a boil.

3. Serve while hot with the onion sauce on the side.

Beef Pot Pie

Ingredients:

- 2 onions (sliced)
- Salt and pepper to taste
- Chopped parsley
- 6 potatoes (peeled and thinly sliced)
- 2 pounds stewing beef

For the pot pie dough

- 1 egg (beaten)
- Milk
- 2 cups flour
- A dash of salt

Directions:

1. Prepare the pot pie dough. Add a dash of salt to 2 cups of flour and add the beaten egg. Gradually add milk as you mix until the dough becomes stiff. Transfer to a floured surface, roll out thinly, and cut into 2-inch squares.

2. Slice the meat into small cubes, and put them in the pot over medium-high flame. Cover them with enough water and add seasonings. Boil until the meat is cooked and tender.

3. Once cooked, add a layer of potatoes and onions, sprinkle with parsley, and place a layer of the pieces of dough. Repeat the process until you have used the remaining ingredients with a dough layer on top. Cover the pot and leave it to boil for 20

minutes.

Chicken Fricassee

Ingredients:

- 2 cups water
- Boiled rice
- A pinch of sage
- A pinch of thyme
- A pinch of celery salt
- 1 whole chicken (chopped)
- 12 white onions
- 2 tablespoons butter
- 2 tablespoons flour
- 1 egg yolk for the gravy

Directions:

1. Place the flour in a shallow bowl and roll the meat until all sides are covered.

2. Put butter in a pan over medium-high flame. Once melted, cook the coated chicken pieces until browned. Add the rest of the ingredients. Check and add water as needed to ensure about 2 cups of fluid will remain in the dish once it's cooked.

3. Prepare the gravy. Mix an egg yolk with 3 tablespoons of the cooking liquid. Stir until combined. Stir into the pan and leave to simmer for 5 minutes.

4. Scoop the dish on top of cooked rice before serving.

· · ·

Chicken Baked in Cream

Ingredients:

- 1/2 cup flour
- 3 tablespoons butter
- 1 whole chicken (chopped)
- Salt and pepper to taste
- 1 1/2 cups sour cream

Directions:

1. Generously rub the meat with salt and pepper, and dredge each piece in flour.

2. Melt butter in a pan over medium flame, and cook the meat until all sides are browned.

3. Transfer the leftover from the pan to a bowl and turn it into a gravy. Set aside.

4. Transfer the meat to a casserole, add cream, and cover before baking in a preheated oven at 350 degrees for 2 hours.

5. Serve the dish along with the gravy.

Schnitzel Meat

Ingredients:

- 1 onion (minced)
- Salt and pepper to taste
- 2 carrots (diced)
- Flour
- 2 tablespoons flour
- 2 tablespoons shortening
- 1.5 pounds veal steak (cut into cubes)
- 1 cup tomato juice

Directions:

1. Mix the flour and seasoning in a shallow bowl. Dredge the cubed steak with the mixture.

2. Melt the shortening in a pan over medium-high flame. Place the dredged meat and cook until browned. Transfer them to a platter.

3. Put flour in the pan, and stir as you add the tomato juice. Mix until the sauce is thick. Put the meat back in the pan, and add onion and carrots. Cover the pan, turn the heat to low, and leave to simmer for 45 minutes.

Mock Duck

Ingredients:

- 1 tablespoon butter
- 1 tablespoon minced onion
- Poultry seasoning
- 1 teaspoon salt
- 1/2 cup milk
- 1 round steak (thick)
- 2 eggs
- 2 cups breadcrumbs

Directions:

1. Prepare the dressing. Put the milk and eggs in a bowl, and whisk as you add the breadcrumbs, seasoning, butter, and onion. Mix well until everything is combined

2. Spread the meat on a flat surface and fill it with the dressing. Roll and secure the meat by tying it with a string. Place in a greased pan and bake in a preheated oven at 375 degrees for an hour and 30 minutes.

3. Remove the string before slicing.

Boova Shenkel (Dutch Meat Rolls)

Ingredients:

- 1 onion (chopped)
- 1/2 cup milk
- Salt and pepper to taste
- 2 1/2 cups flour
- Small cubes of hard bread
- 2 1/2 pounds beef
- 3 eggs
- 2 tablespoons minced parsley
- 3 tablespoons butter
- 10 potatoes (peeled, thinly sliced, and steamed)
- 1 tablespoon shortening
- 2 teaspoons baking powder

Directions:

1. Season the meat with salt and pepper before putting it in a pot with boiling water. Leave to cook for 2 hours over medium-high flame.

2. Put the baking powder, flour, shortening, and half a teaspoon of salt in a bowl. Knead until the dough becomes stiff. Transfer to a flat surface and cut into 12 circles around 10 inches in diameter.

3. In another bowl, put the steamed potatoes, onions, eggs, 2 tablespoons of butter, and parsley. Add salt and pepper, and mix until combined. Scoop a mixture at the center of each dough. Fold the dough and secure the edges by pressing.

4. Scoop out the excess fat from the pot with meat

and set aside. Put the filled dough in the pot, cover, and leave to cook for half an hour.

5. Put a tablespoon of the excess fat, plus a table-spoon of butter into a pan over medium flame. Add the cubed bread and stir until browned. Add milk and mix well.

6. Transfer the meat rolls to a plate and drizzle with the milk and bread mixture on top.

Hygge Recipes for Pancakes and Bread
Apple Pancakes
Ingredients:

- 2 tablespoons butter
- 1 cup milk
- 1 cup flour
- 1/4 teaspoon nutmeg
- 1/4 teaspoon salt
- 1 teaspoon vanilla
- 2 Granny Smith apples (peeled, cored, and chopped)
- 6 eggs

Directions:

1. Put the eggs in a blender, and add the nutmeg, flour, vanilla, milk, and salt. Process until combined.

2. Preheat a cast-iron skillet for 5 minutes and add 2 tablespoons of butter. Fry the apples for 3 minutes before adding the blended mixture.

3. Transfer the skillet to a preheated oven at 475 degrees and bake for 15 minutes. Change the temperature to 425 degrees and bake for 8 more minutes.

4. Add powdered sugar and syrup or jam on top, slice the pancakes into wedges, and serve.

Pumpkin Pancakes

Ingredients:

- 1 1/4 cups milk
- 1/2 cup canned pumpkin
- 1/4 teaspoon cinnamon
- 1 egg (beaten)
- 1 cup flour
- 1/8 teaspoon nutmeg
- 1/8 teaspoon ginger
- 2 tablespoons melted
- 2 tablespoons shortening
- 2 tablespoons sugar
- A pinch of baking soda

Directions:

1. Put flour, spices, sugar, and soda in a bowl and mix until combined.

2. In another bowl, put milk, egg, pumpkin, and shortening, and mix well. Gradually add to the flour mixture and mix until smooth.

3. Preheat a greased griddle. Transfer the mixture and bake in a preheated oven at 425 degrees for 10 minutes. Turn the griddle to the other side and continue baking for 10 more minutes.

3. Serve hot topped with powdered sugar and butter.

German Egg Pancakes

Ingredients:

- 5 eggs (separate yolks from the whites)
- 1 cup sifted flour
- 1/2 cup milk

Directions:

1. Put the yolks in a bowl and beat until light. Gradually add flour and milk as you mix. Continue mixing until smooth.

2. Mix the egg whites until firm. Fold this into the egg and flour mixture, ad transfer to a greased griddle. Put the griddle in a preheated oven at 425 degrees and bake for 10 minutes. Turn on the other side and continue baking for 10 more minutes.

3. Top with jelly or jam, and serve while hot.

Fastnachts (Raised Doughnuts)

Ingredients:

For the sponge

- 1 cake yeast
- 2 cups lukewarm water
- 4 scant cups flour (sifted)

For the dough

- 1 1/2 teaspoons salt
- 1/3 cup sugar
- 5 cups flour
- 2 eggs
- 1/2 cup shortening
- 1/2 teaspoon ground nutmeg

Directions:

1. Prepare the batter the night before you cook the doughnuts. Soak the yeast in lukewarm water for 20 minutes, add flour, and mix well until the mixture becomes a thick batter. Transfer to a greased bowl and cover with a clean and moist cloth. Place in a warm place and leave to rise overnight.

2. Put the sugar, salt, and butter in a bowl and mix until creamed. Transfer the mixture to the risen dough, along with the spices and eggs. Knead the dough until soft. You can gradually add flour as needed or until the dough becomes manageable. Cover and leave for second proofing.

3. Transfer the dough to a floured surface before

rolling and cutting using a doughnut cutter. Cover and allow to rise until each piece doubles in size.

4. Heat the shortening in a deep pan over medium flame. Place the doughnuts in the oil when it reaches 375 degrees and deep fry each piece. Transfer to a platter lined with paper towels to remove excess oils.

5. Sprinkle with powdered sugar and serve at once.

Basic Muffins

Ingredients:

- 5 teaspoons baking soda
- 2 teaspoons vanilla
- 4 cups buttermilk
- 1 cup oil
- 15 ounces raisin bran
- 5 cups flour
- 3 cups sugar
- 2 teaspoons allspice
- 2 teaspoons salt

Directions:

1. Put all the dry ingredients – flour, raisin bran, sugar, salt, allspice, and baking soda, in a bowl and mix until combined.

2. Put all the wet ingredients – buttermilk, oil, and vanilla, in another bowl, and mix until combined. Gradually combine the dry and wet ingredients.

3. Fill each greased muffin tin with the batter up to 3/4 full. Put them in a preheated oven at 375 degrees and bake for 20 minutes.

Blueberry Muffins

Ingredients:

- 1/2 teaspoon salt
- 3/4 cup sugar
- 1/3 cup butter
- 2 level cups flour
- 1 egg (lightly beaten)
- 1 cup blueberries
- 1 cup milk
- 4 level teaspoons baking powder

Directions:

1. Put the sugar and butter in a bowl and mix until creamed. Stir in the egg and milk, and add the sifted flour and baking powder. Mix well before folding in the blueberries.

2. Fill each muffin tin with the batter up to 3/4 full. Place them in a preheated oven at 375 degrees and bake for 20 minutes.

Bran Muffins

Ingredients:

- 1 egg (beaten)
- 1/2 teaspoon salt
- 3 1/2 teaspoons baking powder
- 1 cup flour
- 1 cup bran
- 2 tablespoons melted shortening
- 2 tablespoons brown sugar
- 1/3 cup milk

Directions:

1. In a bowl, put the sifted flour, salt, and baking powder. Add bran and sugar, and mix until combined.

2. In another bowl, put the melted shortening, beaten egg, and milk, and mix well. Combine the two mixtures.

3. Transfer batter to lightly greased muffin pans. Place them in a preheated oven at 425 degrees and bake for 25 minutes.

～

Hygge Recipes for Cookies
Fruit and Nut Cookies
Ingredients:

- 1 cup chopped nuts
- 1 cup shortening
- 1/2 cup chopped currants
- 1/2 cup chopped raisins
- 1 1/2 tablespoons hot water
- 1 1/2 cups sugar
- 3 1/2 cups flour
- 3 eggs
- 1 teaspoon baking soda
- 1 teaspoon salt
- 1 teaspoon cinnamon

Directions:

1. Put the sugar and shortening in a bowl and mix until creamed. Add the eggs and mix until fluffy.

2. Dissolve the baking soda in hot water before adding it to the egg mixture. Mix well until combined

3. In another bowl, sift the flour, cinnamon, and salt. Put half of the mixture into the creamed mixture and mix well. Gently fold in the chopped nuts and fruits before adding the remaining flour mixture. Mix thoroughly.

4. Scoop a teaspoon of the batter for each cookie and arrange them on a greased tray Put the tray in a preheated oven at 350 degrees and bake for 15 minutes.

· · ·

Dutch Almond Cookies

Ingredients:

- 1/2 cup ground blanched almonds
- 1/2 cup white sugar
- 1/2 teaspoon vanilla
- 2 eggs
- 3 cups flour
- 1 cup brown sugar
- 1 cup shortening
- 1/4 teaspoon soda
- 1/4 teaspoon nutmeg
- 1/4 teaspoon salt
- 1/4 teaspoon cinnamon

Directions:

1. Put the sugars and shortening in a bowl, and mix until creamed. Add the eggs and sifted dry ingredients, and mix until well combined. Fold in the chopped blanched almonds.

2. Transfer batter to a waxed paper and roll like a log. Leave in the fried for 2 hours.

3. Peel off the waxed paper and thinly slice the dough. Arrange them on a greased cookie sheet. Place in a preheated oven and bake at 425 degrees for 10 minutes.

Soft Chocolate Chip Cookies

Ingredients:

- 1 12-ounce bag chocolate chips
- 2 eggs
- 1/2 cup shortening
- 2 1/2 cups flour
- 1 teaspoon baking powder
- 3/4 teaspoon baking soda (dissolved in 1/2 cup of milk)
- 1 cup of sugar

Directions:

1. Put the sugar and shortening in a bowl and mix until creamed. Add the baking soda and milk mixture flour, and the eggs, and mix until combined. Gently fold in the chocolate chips.

2. Scoop a teaspoon of the dough for each cookie and arrange them on a greased tray. Place it in a preheated oven at 400 degrees and bake for 12 minutes.

Oatmeal Cookies

Ingredients:

- 1 cup sour milk
- 1 cup peanuts
- 2 tablespoons baking powder
- 2 tablespoons baking soda
- 1/2 cup dark molasses
- 1 1/2 cups raisins
- 1 1/2 cups lard
- 3 eggs (beaten), plus 1 egg (for brushing)
- 6 cups flour
- 3 cups sugar
- 2 1/2 cups oatmeal
- 1 teaspoon salt
- 1 teaspoon cinnamon
- 1 teaspoon nutmeg

Directions:

1. Sift to combine flour, cinnamon, baking powder, salt, and nutmeg in a bowl. Mix in the sugar, oatmeal, and lard.

2. Grind the peanuts and raisins before adding them to the mixture.

3. In another bowl, mix the baking soda and sour milk until dissolved. Add the beaten eggs and molasses. Mix well before adding to the dry ingredients. Chill for an hour.

4. Shape the cookies and arrange them on a greased tray. Brush the top of the cookies with beaten

egg before placing in a preheated oven at 375 degrees. Bake for 15 minutes.

Christmas Butter Cookies

Ingredients:

- 1/2 cup packed brown sugar
- 2 1/4 cups sifted flour
- 1 cup softened butter

Directions:

1. Put the butter in a bowl and mix until it has a consistency similar to whipped cream. Continue beating as you gradually add the sugar and flour. Mix well.

2. Transfer the dough to a waxed paper, wrap, and chill for at least 5 hours.

3. Put the dough on a floured surface before kneading, rolling, and cutting the cookies. Arrange the pieces on a greased tray. Place in a preheated oven at 350 degrees and bake for 12 minutes.

You can decorate the cookies depending on the occasion. You can also drizzle the top with sugar glaze, add butter icing, nuts, or candied fruits.

Pfeffernusse

Ingredients:

- 1/2 teaspoon baking soda
- 1/2 teaspoon cinnamon
- 1/2 pound powdered sugar
- 1/4 teaspoon salt
- 1/4 teaspoon cloves
- 1/4 teaspoon nutmeg
- 2 cups flour
- 3 eggs
- 1 lemon (juice and rind)

Directions:

1. Whisk the eggs in a bowl, and continue mixing as you gradually add the powdered sugar, grated rind, and lemon juice.

2. In another bowl sift the following twice: flour, spices, salt, and baking soda before adding to the egg mixture. Mix until the dough becomes smooth. Cover the bowl and refrigerate for 4 hours.

3. Transfer to a floured surface before rolling. Make long sticks with the same length as your fingers. Cut each stick into smaller pieces and arrange them on a greased tray. Place in a preheated oven at 425 degrees and bake for 12 minutes.

Hygge Pie Recipes
Sour Cream Raisin Pie
Ingredients:

- 2 cups ground raisins
- 1/4 teaspoon nutmeg
- 3/4 teaspoon cinnamon
- 1/8 teaspoon salt
- 1 cup thick sour cream
- 1 cup of sugar
- 3 eggs (slightly beaten)
- 1 unbaked pie shell

Directions:

1. Place the pie shell on an even surface.

2. Put the remaining ingredients in a bowl, and mix thoroughly until combined. Pour into the pie shell and spread until even. Place in a preheated oven at 450 degrees and bake for 15 minutes. Change the temperature to 350 degrees and continue baking for half an hour.

Rivel (Crumb) Pie

Ingredients:

- 1 cup flour
- 1 pastry shell
- 2 tablespoons molasses (optional)
- 1/2 cup shortening (mixed with butter)
- 1/2 cup sugar

Directions:

1. Place the pastry shell on an even surface.

2. Put the remaining ingredients in a bowl and mix with your hands until crumbly. Transfer to the pastry shell and spread evenly. Add the molasses on top, if using, and put in a preheated oven at 400 degrees. Bake for 30 minutes.

Black Walnut Pie

Ingredients:

- 1 1/4 cups dark corn syrup
- 1 1/2 cups water
- 1 1/2 cups sugar
- 2 pie crusts
- 3 tablespoons flour
- 1 cup chopped black walnuts
- 4 eggs

Directions:

1. Beat the eggs in a bowl until foamy. Gradually add sugar as you mix. Fold in the flour, and then add water and corn syrup. Mix well.

2. Sprinkle the chopped black walnuts on your prepared crusts, and add the filling. Place in a preheated oven at 400 degrees and bake for 3 minutes. Change the temperature to 350 degrees and continue baking for half an hour.

Cottage Cheese Pie

Ingredients:

- 1/2 cup sugar
- 1/4 teaspoon cinnamon
- 1/4 teaspoon salt
- 2 tablespoons flour
- 1/2 teaspoon lemon rind (grated)
- 1 pie crust
- 1 1/2 cups cottage cheese
- 2 eggs (separate yolks from the whites, beat the whites until frothy)
- 2 cups milk

Directions:

1. Mix the cottage cheese, spices, sugar, lemon rind, salt, and flour in a bowl. Add the beaten egg yolks and mix until well combined. Add milk and the beaten egg whites as you stir.

2. Put the filling to the pie crust and place in a preheated oven at 350 degrees. Bake for an hour.

Lemon Custard Pie

Ingredients:

- 2 tablespoons flour
- A pinch of salt
- 1/2 cup sugar
- 1 1/2 cups milk
- 2 eggs (separate the yolks from the whites)
- 1 pie shell
- 1 lemon (juice and rind)

Directions:

1. Put the salt, flour, and sugar in a bowl, and mix well.

2. In another bowl, beat the egg yolks, lemon juice, and rind. Add the flour mixture and milk as you mix. Continue mixing until combined

3. Beat the egg whites until stiff, and gently fold them into the mixture. Pour the filling into the pie shell and place in a preheated oven at 425 degrees. Bake for 15 minutes. Change the temperature to 350 degrees and continue baking for 15 minutes.

Schnitz Pie (Dried apples)

Ingredients:

- 1 pie crust, plus lattice strips
- 2 tablespoons cinnamon
- 1 orange (juice and rind)
- 1 pound dried apples (Schnitz)
- 2 cups sugar

Directions:

1. Prepare the dried apples the night before baking by soaking them in water.

2. Place the soaked dried apples in a saucepan over a medium flame the next day, and cover with water. Add the orange rind and juice, and mix well. Boil for several minutes or until soft. Remove the liquid and transfer the apples to a bowl. Mix with cinnamon and sugar.

3. Lightly grease the bottom of the pie crust with butter. Transfer the filling and put the lattice strips on top. Place in a preheated oven at 450 degrees and bake for 10 minutes. Change the temperature setting to 350 degrees and continue baking for half an hour.

Hygge Drinks
Glogg (Spiced Mulled Wine)
Serves: 6

Ingredients:

- 6-ounce (1/8) package blanched almonds (slivered)
- 15-ounce (1/8) package dark raisins
- 1 tablespoon, plus 1/2 teaspoon white sugar
- 8-inch square cheesecloth
- 3-inch strip orange peel
- 3/8 whole cloves
- 1/8 cinnamon stick (small)
- 1/4 whole cardamom pods (cracked)
- 750 ml bottle of bourbon whiskey (100 proof)
- 750 ml bottle port wine

Directions:

1. Put port wine in a pot with a lid over medium flame. Add rum and bourbon and heat until below simmering.

2. Place the orange peel, cloves, cinnamon stick, and cardamom in a cheesecloth. Gather the cloth and tie to secure the contents.

3. Be gentle in lighting the wine mixture once it is hot but not boiling. Use a long-handled match in the process.

4. Add the sugar to the flames and allow it to burn for a minute. Cover the pan with its lid to put

out the flames, and remove it from the stove. Leave for 10 minutes with its lid on until cool.

5. Steep the cheesecloth with the spices and add almonds and raisins to the wine mixture. Leave for an hour.

6. Strain and reserve the almonds and raisins.

7. Put the glogg in a pan and heat over a low-medium flame for 5 minutes when ready to serve. Ladle into cups and top with a little amount of the steeped almonds and raisins.

You can store the glogg up to a year by transferring it to a bottle, cover it tightly, and keep in a cool dark place. You can store the steeped almonds and raisins for up to a year by placing them in a covered bowl, which you will keep refrigerated until ready to use.

Butter Tea with Himalayan Salt

Serves: 2

Ingredients:

- 1 tablespoon butter (grass-fed)
- 1/3 cup half-and-half
- 1/2 teaspoon Himalayan salt
- 4 tablespoon brown or raw sugar (optional)
- 2 cups water
- 1 nugget of fine tea

Directions:

1. Boil water over medium flame and add tea. Once it boils, turn the heat to low and leave to simmer for 10 minutes. Allow to cool a little.

2. Transfer tea to a blender. Add butter, half-and-half, and salt. Blend until frothy.

3. Transfer to your serving cups and enjoy.

Earl Grey Tea Latte with Rose

Serves: 2

Ingredients:

For the tea

- 4 teaspoons rose syrup
- 1 cup whole milk
- 1 tablespoon dried rose petals (edible)
- 2 tablespoons Earl Grey loose leaf tea
- 1 cup boiling water
- Edible rose dust and rose petals (for garnishing)

For the rose syrup

- 1/2 cup dried rose petals (edible)
- 1/4 cup water
- 1/2 cup sugar

Directions:

1. Prepare the rose syrup. Put water and sugar in a saucepan over medium flame. Stir until the sugar dissolves. Remove pan from the stove and place the rose petals. Leave for 5 minutes to steep. Strain the syrup and set it aside.

2. Steep the rose petals and Earl Grey tea in boiling water for 5 minutes.

3. Place milk and rose syrup in a mug and mix using a frother until foamy.

4. Fill half of your mug with tea and half with steamed milk. Garnish with rose dust and serve.

. . .

Creamy Latte with Salted Peanut Butter Cookie

Serves: 1

Ingredients:

For the cookies

- Sea salt (for sprinkles)
- 1/4 teaspoon salt
- 1 teaspoon vanilla extract
- 1 egg yolk
- 1/4 cup loosely packed light brown sugar
- 1/4 cup granulated sugar
- 1/2 cup creamy peanut butter

For the latte

- Steamed whole milk
- 2 espresso shots
- Cookie crumbles
- 1 teaspoon light brown sugar
- 1 tablespoon creamy peanut butter (add more for garnishing)

Directions:

1. Prepare the cookies. In a bowl, put salt, vanilla, egg yolk, sugar, brown sugar, and peanut butter. Mix well.

2. Divide the dough into 2 tablespoons for each cookie. Arrange in a baking sheet and flatten each piece using a fork. Bake in a

preheated oven at 350 degrees F for 12 minutes. Allow to cool.

3. Place 2 espresso shots in a mug and brew. Add the brown sugar and peanut butter whole hot. Mix well. Crumble half of a cookie and add to the latte. Mix well. Add steamed whole milk and stir in more crumbled cookie depending on your preference.

4. Serve the beverage along with the baked cookies.

Beetroot Latte with Ginger

Serves: 1

Ingredients:

- 2 teaspoons of your preferred sweetener
- 1/4 teaspoons ground ginger
- 1 teaspoon beetroot powder
- 1/2 cup of your preferred steamed milk

Directions:

1. Place ground ginger and beetroot powder in a mug. Add a little amount of hot water, and whisk until the mixture has the consistency of a paste.

2. Put the rest of the hot water and add the sweetener. Whisk until combined and dissolved. Add the steamed milk, gently mix, and serve.

Slow-Cooked Gingerbread Latte

Serves 3

Ingredients:

- 1 teaspoon ginger
- 1 teaspoon nutmeg
- 1 tablespoon cinnamon
- 1 1/2 cups half-and-half or creamer
- 1 tablespoon molasses
- 5 cups water
- 10 teaspoons espresso powder (instant)
- Gingerbread candies (optional)
- Whipped cream (optional)

Directions:

1. Put 5 cups of boiling water in the slow cooker and add the espresso powder. Add spices, creamer, and molasses. Mix well.

2. Cook for 45 minutes on a high setting.

3. Transfer to cups and top with whipped cream, gingerbread candies, or a sprinkle of cinnamon powder.

**Slow-Cooked   Cinnamon   Latte   with   White
Chocolate**

Serves: 2

Ingredients:

- 1/4 teaspoon cinnamon
- 1 teaspoon vanilla
- 11 ounces white chocolate chips
- 1 cinnamon stick
- 1 cup half-and-half
- 5 cups brewed coffee

Directions:

1. Put everything in a slow cooker. Cook for 3 hours. Transfer to mugs and top with your preferred garnishing. You can use whipped cream, cinnamon sticks, or cinnamon sprinkles.

Chai Latte with Pumpkin Spice

Serves: 2

Ingredients:

- 5 tablespoons pumpkin pie spice creamer
- 2 flavored tea bags (chai blend)
- 2/3 cup milk
- 3/4 teaspoon cornstarch
- 3 tablespoons real pumpkin puree
- 1 cup water
- Cinnamon sticks (for garnishing)

Directions:

1. Put milk, cornstarch, pumpkin puree, and water in a blender. Mix until combined and smooth. Transfer to a small pan over medium flame.

2. Whisk often as you let it simmer for 2 minutes or until the mixture is thick and creamy.

3. Place a tea bag in each serving cup. Pour the boiled pumpkin milk mixture, and leave for 5 minutes to steep.

4. Discard the tea bags, and add 2 1/2 creamer o each mug. Mix and taste. Add sweetener, if desired.

Vegan Latte with Chai

Serves: 1

Ingredients:

- 1/8 teaspoon finely ground black pepper
- 1/8 teaspoon ground cloves
- 1/8 teaspoon ground cardamom
- 1/4 teaspoon ground ginger
- 1/4 teaspoon ground cinnamon
- 1/4 teaspoon vanilla extract
- 1 tablespoon maple syrup
- 1 black tea bag
- 1 cup unsweetened vanilla plant-based milk (such as oat, rice, hemp, coconut, or almond)
- Garnishing of choice (cinnamon stick, a sprinkle of cinnamon, or star anise)

Directions:

1. Microwave milk for 2 to 8 minutes on a high setting.

2. Place the teabag in the hot milk and leave to steep for 2 minutes. Discard the teabag.

3. Transfer tea to a blender, and add the rest of the ingredients. Process until frothy.

4. Transfer drink to a mug, and garnish before serving.

Hojicha Latte with Cinnamon
Serves: 1
Ingredients:

- 1/4 cup frothed milk
- 1/2 teaspoon vanilla extract
- 1/4 teaspoon cinnamon (add more for garnishing)
- 1 tablespoon honey
- 1 tablespoon Hojicha
- 1 cup boiling water

Directions:

1. Brew the tea for 7 minutes. For every tablespoon of tea leaves, you will need a cup of boiling water.

2. Put vanilla, cinnamon, and honey in your mug. Transfer the brewed tea and mix until combined. Add the frothed milk and garnish with cinnamon.

Lavender Latte
Serves: 2
Ingredients:

- Water
- 3 teaspoons instant coffee (for each cup)
- 1 1/2 teaspoons dried lavender flowers
- 600 ml milk

Directions:

1. Put the dried lavender flowers and milk on a pan over medium flame. Stir and leave to boil. Strain and allow to cool a little. Mix using a milk frother.

2. Put coffee in each cup and add 1 cm deep of hot water. Pour the lavender milk on top.

Always remember that in hygge, you have to enjoy the process of food preparation and these dishes are best served when shared.

AFTERWORD

I hope this book was able to shed light on hygge and how you can incorporate its techniques into your daily life. Hygge aims to make you happier without imposing anything. It gives you a chance to slow down, and in the process, pick up some new hobbies and skills. It is up to you how you will make it work and what techniques will fit your life.

The next step is to relieve yourself of anything dragging you down and stop making your life complicated. Be happy. Go hygge.

I wish you the best of luck!

Danielle Kristiansen

Printed in Great Britain
by Amazon

19868650R00098